Clark Gable, in Pictures

Clark Gable, in Pictures

Candid Images of the Actor's Life

CHRYSTOPHER J. SPICER

McFarland & Company, Inc., Publishers
Jefferson, North Carolina, and London

LIBRARY OF CONGRESS CATALOGUING-IN-PUBLICATION DATA

Spicer, Chrystopher J.
Clark Gable, in pictures : candid images of
the actor's life / Chrystopher J. Spicer.
p.   cm.
Includes bibliographical references and index.

ISBN 978-0-7864-4964-4
illustrated case binding : 60# alkaline paper ∞

1. Gable, Clark, 1901–1960— Portraits.   I. Title.
PN2287.G3S76 2012   791.4302'8092 — dc23   [B]   2011033864

BRITISH LIBRARY CATALOGUING DATA ARE AVAILABLE

On the front cover: Clark looks happy and relaxed
with both camera and prize, California, 1934
(courtesy Carole Sampeck/Carole Lombard Archive)

Manufactured in the United States of America

*McFarland & Company, Inc., Publishers
Box 611, Jefferson, North Carolina 28640
www.mcfarlandpub.com*

To my late friends,

Barry "Baz" Flanagan
with whom I went to the movies,

and

Cammie King (Bonnie Blue Butler) Conlon
who remembered the movies with me

Contents

Acknowledgments

Many of these photographs did not come to this collection as 8 × 10 black-and-white glossies, sharply focused and clearly lit. Some were of considerable age and were probably taken with a Box Brownie or vest-pocket Kodak, and they looked it. So, I would first like to express my profound gratitude to my talented and very patient wife, Marci, who spent many hours digitally restoring and enhancing many of these photographs in order for them to be considered for publication.

I would also like to express my special gratitude to a group of people who sometimes found themselves drawn into this project before they realized it to help me research information that was otherwise geographically out of my reach: Carole Sempak of the Carole Lombard Archive; Ken Harbour, historian for the 351st Bomb Group (Heavy) Association and co-author of *The 351st Bomb Group in WWII*; Philip Hulse from the *Argonaut III* and his son Alvin; Su Kim Chung, Manuscripts Librarian, Special Collections at the University of Nevada Las Vegas Library; and Charles B. Wallace from the Harrison County Historical Society, Cadiz, Ohio. I would also like to thank Nan Mattern and Jackie Rocchi from the Clark Gable Foundation and Birth Home Museum in Cadiz, Ohio, for their friendship and ongoing support over many years.

This remarkable collection of photographs would have been impossible to assemble without the assistance and permission of the following people, and so for their contribution I would like to express my gratitude to:

MUSEUMS, COLLECTIONS AND ASSOCIATIONS

At the 3 Dog Garage, Boyertown, Pennsylvania: general manager Chris Liebenberg and William Andresen from Andresen Advertising, Exton, Pennsylvania.

At the 91st Bomb Group Memorial Association: Jim Shepherd, president, and Gordon Alton.

At the 303rd Bomb Group Memorial Association: Gary L. Moncur, historian.

At the AACA Museum, Hershey, Pennsylvania: Jeffrey Bliemeister, curator.

At the Addis Historical Society, Louisiana: Jocelyn Gauthreaux.

At the *Akron Beacon-Journal*, Akron, Ohio: Mark Price.

At the Akron-Summit County Public Library Special Collections, Ohio: Mary Plazo, librarian.

At the High Museum of Art, Atlanta, Georgia: Berry Lowden Perkins, curatorial assistant.

At the Auburn Cord Duesenberg Automobile Museum, Auburn, Indiana: Jon Bill, archivist.

At The Bahre Collection, Paris Hill, Maine: Jeff Orwig.

At Bonhams & Butterfields, U.S.: Alec Rapalski, Digital Production Dept.; D. Levi Morgan, public relations; Lisa Gerhauser, vice-president and general counsel.

At Bonhams & Goodman, Australia: Charlotte Stanes, head of marketing and media.

At the Catalina Island Museum Research Center, Avalon, California: Christina Butler, collections intern.

At Classic Auto Sports Ltd., Inverkeilor, Angus, Scotland: David Barnett.

At Country House Inns: Erik R. Johnson, operations support manager; Kirt Davis, innkeeper, Weasku Inn, Grants Pass, Oregon.

At Glenmoor Gathering of Significant Automobiles, Canton, Ohio: David W. Schultz, executive director, and Myron Vernis.

At HMS Bounty Organization LLC, Smithtown, New York: Tracie Simonin, director, and Margaret Ramsey, former executive director.

At Indianapolis Motor Speedway Photo Operations, Indianapolis, Indiana: Mary Ellen Loscar.

At *Jaguar Magazine*, Australia: Les Hughes.

At JD Classics, Wycke Hill, Maldon, Essex, UK: Derek Hood and Micky Collins.

At the Kings England Press, Goldthorpe, Rotherham, UK: poet Deborah Tyler-Bennett, and editor and founder Steve Rudd.

At the Leopold Retirement Residence, Bellingham, Washington: Ginger Oppenheimer, marketing director.

At Make It Happen Marketing LLC: Karen Fronek, president.

At Montgomery Communications, New York City: Virginia Haynes Montgomery and Jo C. Tu.

At Motorcycle USA, Medford, Oregon: Bart Madson, managing editor.

At the Mount Dora Museum of Speed and Classic Dreamcars, Mt. Dora, Florida: Kerry Bogard.

At the Music Box @ Fonda, Hollywood Blvd., Los Angeles: Sarah Quigley, event-sales manager.

At the National Skeet Shooting Association: Don Snyder, executive director, and at the NSSA-NSCA Museum, San Antonio, Texas: Mike Brazzell and Jim Harris.

At the Naval History Archive/NHF Photos: Frank Arre.

At the New England Air Museum, Windsor Locks, Connecticut: Mike Speciale, executive director, and Barbe LaPierre, administrator, 58th Bomb Wing Memorial.

At the Oundle School, Oundle, Peterborough, UK: Lindsey Crosswell, Michael Downes, archivist Steven Forge, and the late Barry Smith.

At the Pacific County Historical Society, South Bend, Washington: Karla Webber and Charles Summer.

At Parkhurst Art Galleries, San Pedro, Los Angeles: Warren Hsiao, vice-president, and the late and much-missed Violet Parkhurst.

At the Pebble Beach Company, Pebble Beach, California: Neal Hotelling, historian.

At www.riverboatdaves.com, the James E. York Post Card Collection: Riverboat Dave.

At Carr-Hartley Safaris, Nairobi, Kenya: Judy and Roy Carr-Hartley.

At Special Collections, University of Nevada Reno Libraries: Donnie Curtis.

At Success Communications Inc.: Maria Writesel.

At the University of Manitoba, Canada: Dr. L. Gordon Goldsborough, director of Delta Marsh Field Station.

At U.S. 8th Air Force Little Friends, UK: Peter Randall.
At the Whatcom Museum Photo Archives, Bellingham, Washington: Jeff Jewell.
At Woodies USA, Cave Creek, Arizona: Wes Aplanalp.

INDIVIDUALS

Dennis Adler, Kinsey Barnard, Don Boyd, Michael Brent, Lou Brooks, Richard Calver, Cammie Conlon, William Constable, Ashley Copeland, Bill Counter, Bob Davies, Robert F. Dorr, John Elliott, John Elmgreen, Tammi Fabre, Kit Foster, Gregory Gibson, John Gillespie, Victoria Graham, Alvin Hulse, Colleen Kane, Tom Knight, Dr. Norman Lambert, Larry Lawrence, the Lokken family, Kathleen Marcaccio, John McElwee, Terry McGrath, Karl Meek, Bruce Meyer, R. Anna Millman, Thomas Moretti, Michael Randall, Rick School, Thomas P. Smith, Jeff Stafford, Erika Stone, Linda Thompson, Sheryl Todd, John P. Verostek, David Wells, Christi Welter, Mike Williams, Diana Wirt, and Bill Wylde.

Preface

This book has taken me on a journey, as many books do. What started out to be a compilation of photographs from my collection became a journey to photographs in other people's albums and the stories surrounding them. Every life is a story and during the course of his life Clark Gable appeared in so many photographed stories that eventually his life became one. Beneath the surface, though, there were often two versions of that story: the officially photographed studio version and the candid everyday one that appears in many of the photographs in this book. However, on many occasions those two versions would mingle because both private and public photographers would be present.

Because of his popularity, Clark's life in and out of the studio was one of the most photographed of the time. Yet after he had gone, no central archive of documents or photographs about this actor's life survived to ensure that the memory of this man whose acting life had begun on stage during the 1920s, and whose significant movie career spanned over 65 films from the silent era until just before his death, was maintained for the future. Consequently, this project to compile a personal photographic record of him had to cast nets far indeed upon the waters of memory, and so these photographs have come from a wide variety of sources and places, often through the kindness of strangers. Many have never been previously published.

While writing my previous biography (*Clark Gable: Biography, Filmography, Bibliography*, McFarland, 2002), I became interested in the person behind the studio star portraits. I began to look for him through the smaller, more casual lens because it is there within these candid "snapshots" taken with box Brownies and Kodak vest pocket cameras where for me the human being is revealed. There is the friendly, mannered, elegantly sociable yet down-home Clark who enjoyed mingling with people, young and old, from all walks of life, as well as the enthralling raconteur who enjoyed nothing more than sitting down with a small circle of friends to swap a few stories, whether around a campfire or a table at Ciros. Here in these images we can see that infrequently revealed, off-stage Clark: the man at peace canoeing on a lake or proudly holding a fish he's caught, happily sitting behind the wheel of a new car or enjoying himself at the Indianapolis 500. In that sense, then, I have attempted to follow a Clark Gable tradition here by telling some stories.

However, we are not only revealed by our physical selves but also by our possessions and our environment, those inanimate objects with which we surround ourselves that are animated by us. Our houses, cars, furniture, books, occupation and recreation all tell their own stories about us to the observer, so there are some photographs here about Clark in which he is nowhere to be seen. One of his great passions, for example, was unique, expensive and fast cars. He didn't collect them as investments to be stored; they were there to be driven fast, were meticulously cared for by him, were changed often and were frequently customized to his personal taste. Actually, the more you think about that, there is much in Clark's life that can be summed up by his attitude to cars.

He was a man who wore his professional status as the "King of Hollywood" confidently, like one of his tailored outfits. He was the consummate Hollywood career movie star, whose talent was recognized only four years after his major film career had begun with a Best Actor Academy Award for his performance in *It Happened One Night* (1934). He became one of the MGM studio's most marketable male stars, culminating in his 1939 role as Rhett Butler in *Gone with the Wind*: the ultimate romantic hero who woos the heroine, but who chooses not to take up the offer when he finally wins her. During his career he worked with such famous female actors as Claudette Colbert, Joan Crawford, Greta Garbo, Jean Harlow, Vivien Leigh, Sophia Loren, Myrna Loy, Marilyn Monroe, Norma Shearer, Gene Tierney, and Lana Turner, as well as male actors such as Lionel Barrymore, Wallace Beery, Burt Lancaster, and Spencer Tracy. His range of roles varied from the villainous kidnapping chauffeur in *Night Nurse* to the rugged and steamy romance of *Red Dust*, from the high-seas heroism of *Mutiny on the Bounty* to singing and dancing in *Idiot's Delight*, from making difficult decisions about fighting a war in *Command Decision* to being a cowboy roping the last mustangs and coping with age in *The Misfits*.

Yet Clark was a private person who always appreciated being able to shut his front door and leave the studio outside. As many a famous person has realized, celebrity status often means conflict between the public and the private persona. One must stay in the public eye or be forgotten, at which point you are no longer a celebrity. But the public eye is an unremitting gaze; it's the Eye of the Basilisk that sees all, to which a celebrity is completely exposed. Privacy by its very nature hints at secrets, hints that the public is being denied that which it most seeks to know, and so the celebrity is caught on the horns of a dilemma. If the fickle public is denied access to what they want to know for too long, they will switch their attention to someone else, and the celebrity who was somebody becomes nobody. Give the public too much information, though, and your privacy is lost at the risk of the public becoming surfeited with your life and still moving on to someone else. You may have gained fame but at the cost of living in a fishbowl. So, remaining a celebrity becomes a Faustian balancing act at which only the most highly trained performers are truly successful. There is no room for mistakes on this tightrope, under which there is no net.

Consequently, Clark developed some excellent rope-walking skills while of course being carefully managed by his studio's public relations people. Nevertheless, he encountered more than a few predators during his career. Women quite literally couldn't keep their hands off him. He had a female fan following, especially during the thirties, who in the extremities of its desire for physical contact with him certainly equaled anything that fans of later rock stars would exhibit. His shirts were torn from his back, his ties from around his neck, his belts from his pants and his shoes from his feet. On at least one occasion, his plane could not take off because women were sitting on the wings; on another, his car was over turned from the weight of women trying to climb in the windows. His hotel rooms had to be inspected before he entered them so that women could be removed from the wardrobes and from under the bed. His used sheets and towels would frequently be quietly sold to demanding female fans — unwashed of course. His fans weren't all women, though; his lack of an undershirt in *It Hap-*

pened One Night reputedly caused a slump in the male underwear industry, and men everywhere copied the Gable moustache and the Gable hat. His Air Force missions prompted a rise in enlistment. He was even popular with criminals and the disenchanted: gangster John Dillinger was famously gunned down by the FBI after emerging from a showing of Gable's *Manhattan Melodrama*, and the FBI kept a covert file of letters addressed to Clark asking for money or threatening blackmail or kidnapping of both him and, later, his wife Carole Lombard. However, in perhaps the ultimate honor, his name became part of common vocabulary: an often-heard question directed at many a would-be suitor or well-dressed man was, "Who do you think you are? Clark Gable!"

Yet at the same time, there was that private human being behind the public star image. While for most of his career one of the highest-paid male actors in Hollywood, for example, Clark was a pragmatic realist who never forgot that fickle public opinion could put him right back on those humble small-town streets from where he had come. He was not a man who liked to display wealth ostentatiously, and he lived in the same relatively plain ranch house for a third of his life. As a star, he maintained a house staff of cook, gardener, valet and personal assistant, yet he was a man grounded in reality who didn't mind getting his own hands dirty, either within the engine of his latest fast car or in the dirt and around the stables of his Encino ranch. He loved being himself with his dogs, horses, guns, cars, small circle of good friends and family. Although his life for many years centered around his work, one of his major career aims was to reach the kind of star status where he could have a clause written into his contract that allowed him to go home at six at night.

While some chronology is inevitable in any biographical work, I've organized these photographs into sections that reflect major aspects of Clark's life in order to shift focus away from a date series to the random moments that reveal the man. These have been numbered to make that important association between the image and the word easier. After all, each of these photographs is a story in itself of a man who was both public and private, both a star and the person Clark Gable.

Chrystopher J. Spicer • Cairns, Australia

Early Life

1   In a soft, comfortable bed under the left-side upper floor window of this unremarkable frame house, Clark Gable was born to William Gable and Adeline J. (also Adelia or Addie) Hershelman at 5:30 A.M. on February 1, 1901. A big baby who grew into a big man, he weighed in at ten-and-a-half pounds. Will was an oil-driller and wildcatter and the newly married Gables had moved to Cadiz the previous year because a new oil field had been discovered just out of town. They had originally lived on the other side of Charleston Street, but not long after Addie became pregnant their landlord decided to re-plaster the house and they had to

1   Photographed by Charles Wallace just before its untimely demolition, this is the original house on Charleston Street in Cadiz, Ohio, in which Clark Gable was born (courtesy Harrison County Historical Society, Ohio).

2 The reconstructed Gable birthplace, now the Clark Gable Birthplace and Museum (courtesy the Gable Archive).

move. Will's co-worker Tom Reese lived with his wife in the bottom floor of this house; Tom knew that the upper floor was vacant, and so Will and Addie were able to move in immediately.

Their new apartment consisted of three main rooms: a living room and bedroom at the front, each about 12 foot square, and a kitchen area at the back off which were a small nursery and pantry. Access to the front and rear doors, however, could only be gained by external stairs, and as winter closed in Addie became increasingly housebound and quite ill. Like many mothers-to-be, though, she was attuned to her unborn child, telling the iceman one morning that she would need extra ice the following day as the baby would be arriving.

Unknown to people around her then, Addie was already terminally ill with an aggressive brain tumor. Her health deteriorated rapidly after the birth, and so in the spring William Gable moved his family into more accessible living quarters on Lincoln Avenue. A short time later, he took Addie back to her family in Pennsylvania.

The Gables' association with the house lost significance over the years. Only a few years after Clark died, it was deemed unsafe and torn down.

2 Fortunately for posterity, people's attitudes about historical significance change with time. On February 1, 1984, a radio talk show host called the Cadiz, Ohio, post office and asked them if they knew it was Clark's birthday and whether the town was doing anything to celebrate it. They didn't and they weren't but some townspeople vowed that situation wouldn't happen again. By the next year, February 1 had been declared Clark Gable Day and the Clark Gable Foundation had been born. In 1986, an inscribed granite monument was installed on what was then the vacant site of his birthplace.

	Name	Date	Place			Parents	No.	
	" Swan Mary M.	1900 / June 14	Cadiz	F	W	Annie A. Wood / A.D. McFarlan	241	
	" McFarland Theodore Edward	1900 / July 16	Cadiz	M	W	Catharine White / L.A. Decker	242	
	" Decker Raymond Morgan	1900 / Dec.11	Cadiz	M	W	Nettie Morgan / J.M. Johnson	243	
	" Johnson Anne Madge	1900 / June 25	Cadiz	F	W	Laura B. Braden / Harry H. Finnical	244	
	" Finnical Esther Elizabeth	1900 / Jan 20	Cadiz	F	W	Jessie M. Anderson / Emmet E. Webb	245	
	" Webb Robert Lois	1900 / Aug.13	Cadiz	M	W	Jennie Farrah / Daniel McDongal	246	
	" McDongal Minnie	1900 / Nov.24	Cadiz	F	W	Minnie Shores / William N. Spencer	247	
/	" Spencer Iva Grace	1900 / Feb.7	No ngham	F	W	Blanche Johnston / Albert Rogers	248	
	" Rogers Myrtle Luella	1901 / Oct.2	Cadiz	F	W	Bertha Palmer / W.E. Dickerson	249	
June 10	Dickerson Kenneth Barrett	1900 / Dec.9	Cadiz	M	W	Mary L. Dickerson / Chas. Hunt	250	
	" Hunt Francis S.	1900 / Oct.22	Cadiz	M	W	Fannie Searrs / J.S. West	251	
	" West Elizabeth	1900 / Jan 14	Cadiz	F	W	Jennie Moore / E.L. Haverfield	252	
	" Haverfield Melvin L.	1901 / Feb.1	Cadiz	M	W	Edna Billwell / Wm. Gable	253	
	" Gable Clark	1901 / Aug.5	Cadiz	M	W	Adelia Hershelman / L.J. Brokaw	254	
	" Brokaw Nellie	1900 / May 7	Cadiz	F	W	Dana Parks / D.E. Fierbaugh	255	
	" Fierbaugh Sarah A.	1900 / Sept.20	Cadiz	F	W	Kittie Sparks / Wm. Sharp	256	
	" Sharp John C.	1900 / Oct.18	Cadiz	M	W	Lydia Stevenson / Geo Harsh	257	
	" Freeman Wm. Freeman	1900 / Mar.23	Cadiz	M	W	Jessie ?. Freeman / A. Jacobs ?ard	258	
	" Jacobs Bertie	1901 / Feb.27	Cadiz	F	W	Anna Miller / Nosh Blanchard	259	
	" Blanchard Donald R.	1901 / Jan 29	Cadiz	M	C	Susan Alexander / Andrew Brooks	256	
	" Brooks Leander	1901 / Apr.15	Cadiz	M	C	Minnie Burks / John Davis	257	
	" Davis Dorothy L	1900 / Jan 26	Cadiz	F	W	Louise Schneider / Howard Carter	258	
	" Carter Carl Edward	1901	Cadiz	M	C	Mary E. Bolden	259	

3 The typed version of the Harrison County birth register page that shows the entry for Clark Gable's birth (courtesy Harrison County Historical Society, Ohio).

The Foundation felt that Clark deserved more than just a granite slab and, thanks to a $300,000 bequest from Isabelle Clifford, they were eventually able to purchase the property where the original birthplace house had stood. Work then began on a reconstruction of the original house to a design by Jack Harden that would serve as a focal point for remembering Clark Gable. Opened by his son, John Clark Gable, on January 30, 1998, the Clark Gable Birthplace and Museum recreates the upper-floor apartment as it would have looked when the Gable family lived there. It now houses a growing collection of Gable memorabilia and artifacts, including his 1954 Cadillac DeVille and a collection of Carole Lombard memorabilia. It also houses the offices of the Clark Gable Foundation.

3–4 For some reason, Clark's name wasn't recorded in the Harrison County register until June 10, 1901, more than four months after his birth. It's possible that Will had to leave town immediately after the birth to return to work, in which case Addie would have been too ill to venture down those stairs in the middle of a snowy Ohio winter to walk down the steep hill to the county seat building.

As you can see on this page, Clark was one of the rare Hollywood actors who did not change his name for his career. For most of his life, his name remained two simple words: Clark Gable. There was never an official third name. Judging by other registrations, this does not seem to have been an unusual practice at that time; there are at least five other children

CERTIFIED COPY OF BIRTH RECORD

The State of Ohio, ...Harrison...... County.   **Court of Common Pleas
Probate Division**

Date of Record.   June 10th   *A.D.*   1901

No. 254

Name in Full ......Clark Gable......

Date of Birth – Year 1 901 *Month* February   *Day* 1st

Place of Birth – State. Ohio   , *County*. Harrison

City, Town or Township   Cadiz

Sex   Male

Color   White

Name of Father   Wm. Gable

Mother's Maiden Name Adelia Hershelman

Residence of Parents   Cadiz

By whom reported and address   Assessor

The State of Ohio, ...Harrison...... County.

*I the undersigned,
certify that I am Judge of the Court of Common Pleas, Probate Division, within and for said County,
which is a Court of Record; that I am ex-officio Clerk of said Court and by law the custodian of the
records and papers required by law to be kept in said Court; that among others a* Record of Births *was
heretofore required by law to be kept therein; and that said person's birth has been registered according
to law.*
Record of Births, Vol* ...2... *Page* ...107... *now in this office.*

*WITNESS my signature and the seal of said Court,
at* ....Cadiz........ *Ohio, this* ...23rd.
day of ......August......, *19*85

Robert B. Werren
Judge

By ....
Deputy Clerk

William Clark Gable

4 A copy of Clark Gable's birth certificate, certified in 1985 to replace the original which has
long since vanished (courtesy Harrison County Historical Society, Ohio).

in just this section of the page who have only a first and a family name. So, Clark was *not* born William Clark Gable nor did he ever officially change his name to that. For a brief period in his early twenties, mainly when he was in Oregon, he experimented with adding his father's name to his own and consequently was occasionally known as Billy Gable. But by the time he was well-known as a stage actor he'd returned to Clark Gable.

The two columns in the middle of the page in which only letters appear are for gender, on the left, and color. In the original handwritten register where the entry for Clark's name appeared on page 107 (a photograph of which appears in my earlier Gable biography but which has since disappeared), the county clerk originally wrote both M and F in the appropriate gender columns after Clark's name and then crossed them out later, re-writing the M. It wasn't that the clerk had doubts about the Gable masculinity; apparently Dr. John S. Campbell, the local doctor who attended the birth, didn't have the most legible handwriting, and so sometimes a cautious clerk would write both genders into the register alongside names until they could check with Dr. Campbell.

5   Looking at the face of this young mother, you can immediately see Clark's dark, wavy hair, expressive eyes and strong
chin. A striking, dark-eyed brunette, Addie was sensitive and
artistic but you can also see determination and will in the line
of her jaw and the way she carries her head. Addie's grand-
parents, Jacob Hershelman and Elizabeth Hill, had migrated
to the United States from Bavaria by 1833 and then in 1847
had moved, with their children, from New York State to Vernon,
Pennsylvania, where their eldest son John had married Rosetta
Clark (after whom the infant Gable was named). Their family
grew but then Rosetta died when Addie was only 16. As the
eldest daughter, Addie had to take on the responsibility of car-
ing for the family.

5   The only known photo-
graph of Adeline Hershelman
(courtesy Harrison County
Historical Society, Ohio).

Many years later she was still there, well on her way to
spinsterhood in those days, when her life was changed by
meeting Will Gable. This may well have happened through
the matchmaking of her sister who worked at the Kepler
House, a hotel in nearby Meadville. Will, who was about the
same age as Addie, probably stayed there during his periodic
visits back to that town to visit his family. Despite her chance
of marriage, her family may not have been entirely pleased. In this quiet and respectable community, falling for a wildcatter was probably the equivalent of eloping with a riverboat gambler
further south. Not only that, Will was Methodist and the Hershelmans were Roman Catholic.

There is a story that her parents sent her off to Paris to study painting and (they hoped)
to forget Will Gable, only for her to return a year later having decided that her modest talent
did not justify any further investment of the family's money.

Against such odds, they fell in love and were married in 1900, only for her health to
noticeably deteriorate shortly after Clark was born.

6   Like the Hershelmans, the Gables were German emigrants to America who probably
arrived in the late 18th century. Clark's great-grandfather and great-grandmother, John Gable
and Sarah Frankfield, had come west to Crawford County, Pennsylvania, from LeHigh County

over near the Hudson River around 1825. They settled in Meadville where John became a teamster hauling goods between Erie and Pittsburgh. The family eventually grew to seven and in 1852 one of those children, Charles, took over the local Crawford House and went into the hotel business. Twelve years later, he purchased the Sherwood House which he renovated and renamed the Gable House. By now, he and his wife Nancy Stainbrook had five children and needed extra space, and so Charles bought the 170-acre farm of his brother John just outside of town at what is now known as Gable Hill. In time they rounded off the family at ten.

Born in 1870, William Henry Gable was the eighth child in that family. When he was about 17, he evidently decided he wanted to see more of life than what Meadville had to offer and so he left for the Titusville area where oil had been discovered to learn about drilling and the art of "tool dressing": sharpening and replacing drill bits on site in what were frequently very dangerous conditions. It was during one of his trips back to Meadville to see his family that he met Addie.

After they moved to Cadiz, life couldn't have been easy for Addie with Will away for lengthy periods of time, but by the time Clark came along Will was so good at his profession that he had set up business as a freelance oil drilling prospector. So, although their living circumstances might have been humble, they were not poor.

Clark and Will had a life-long relationship full of contrast. While on the one hand the rather gruff, taciturn, practical Will could never quite work out what Clark saw in acting as a career, there's no doubt that he loved him in his own way. He lavished toys on Clark as a child, taught him how to swim, fish, hunt and shoot, and would make sure he had anything he asked for when Clark was ill. He even allowed Clark to keep

6 Clark as a young man photographed together with his father, William Henry Gable, in Akron in 1920 (courtesy Harrison County Historical Society, Ohio).

a stray dog that followed him home one day. When his son later became an actor, though, it was a different world that he could not understand. Even when Clark was making $7500 a week, his father would grumble that it was no job for a guy six feet tall and 195 pounds. Clark constantly sought his approval but, until the day Will died, he refused to be impressed by his son's choice of career.

7–8 As an infant, Clark already had those broad hands, squared face, dark eyebrows and warm expressive eyes that would melt many a heart through the years. Showing early signs of independence, he was soon able to sit up and do things for himself. Without doubt he was his father's pride and joy and the light of his mother's short life.

Addie's health had continued to deteriorate. By April of 1901 she was suffering from involuntary convulsions, her mental condition had declined and her personality had noticeably changed. In her last lucid moments, knowing she was already too ill to witness the occasion, Addie pleaded that Clark be baptized into the Roman Catholic faith. Cadiz, however, was a Protestant community and the nearest priest was some miles away in the next county. Finally a neighbor, John Conway, carried the baby with him over the trail to the Immaculate Conception Church in Dennison where Clark was baptized by Father Patrick M. Heery on July 31.

Will then took Addie back to her home and her father in Pennsylvania where her long agony ended on November 14. She was buried in the Chestnut Corners cemetery where, for some reason, her headstone still records her as having died before the date when Clark was born.

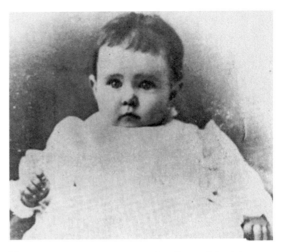

7 Clark at about six months, dressed for his christening (courtesy Harrison County Historical Society, Ohio).

8 Clark's baptismal certificate (courtesy Harrison County Historical Society, Ohio).

Certificate of Baptism

Immaculate Conception Church
DENNISON, OHIO

This is to Certify

That William Clarke Gable
Child of William Gable
and Adelia Hershelman
born in Cadiz Ohio
on the 1 day of February 19 01
was **Baptized**
on the 31 day of July 19 01
According to the Rite of the Roman Catholic Church
by the Rev. P.M. Heery
the Sponsors being John Conway / Mrs. John Conway
as appears from the Baptismal Register of this Church.

Dated March 8, 1968

FR. ADAM F. X. STROMSKI   Pastor

NO. 314 F. J. REMEY CO. INC. N.Y

9   Approximately 20 miles northwest of Cadiz, Dennison might be a small, quiet town of just under 3000 these days but when Clark was a boy it was a boom town. Initially it was selected as a water stop because locomotives had to coal and water every 100 miles and Dennison was 100 miles from either Columbus or Pittsburgh. The town developed from 1865 as the site of the Pittsburgh, Cincinnati & St. Louis Railway (later the Pennsylvania Railroad Company) workshops and yards. During the late 19th and early 20th centuries, the yards and railroad shops spread to occupy 40 acres and employ over 2500 people in the roundhouses and turntables, foundries, workshops and sidings. Although many of the tracks remain, the buildings are mostly gone now except for the restored 1873 depot, now the focus of the Dennison Railroad Depot Museum.

The town's original Immaculate Conception Church was completed in 1871, followed by the adjacent rectory. The congregation must have grown rapidly because the church was enlarged and then dedicated in 1880, and it would have been in this version of the church where Clark was baptized by Father Heery in 1901. Fifteen years later, still during Heery's pastorate, there was the addition of a vaulted sanctuary, two sacristies and a pair of handsome stained glass windows, and this is the church that stands today on the northeast corner of First and Sherman.

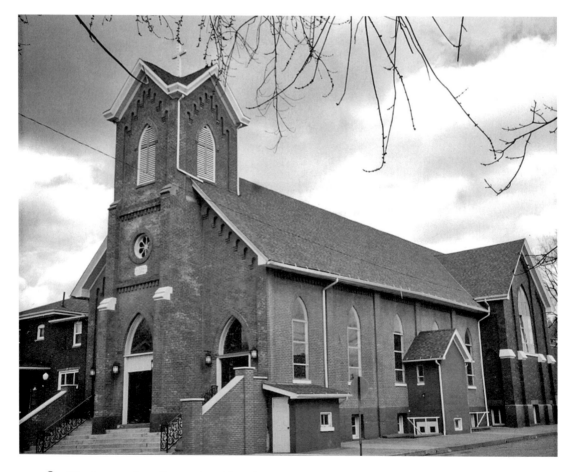

9   **The Immaculate Conception Church in Dennison, Ohio, as it appears today (courtesy the Gable Archive).**

10 Will was faced with a problem: as much as he loved his son, his work took him out into the field and it was no place for a baby, especially with winter coming on. He'd let the business run down over the last few months while trying to take care of Addie, and money must have been low. With no place of his own now, he had to make the difficult decision to leave Clark behind while he went back to work. So he turned "the Kid," as he often liked to call baby Clark, over to the care of Addie's family while he returned to Ohio from where he periodically sent money to provide for his son's care. Clark went to live on a farm with his aunt and uncle, Elizabeth and Tom Hershelman, where by all accounts they loved Clark as their own.

Some time during the summer of 1902, Will Gable found lodging with the Dunlap family in Hopedale, only a few miles east of Cadiz. The Dunlaps had been in this part of the country almost as long as the Gables and Hershelmans; Adam Dunlap had arrived in Harrison County with his wife and family around the turn of the 19th century. Hopedale was enjoying

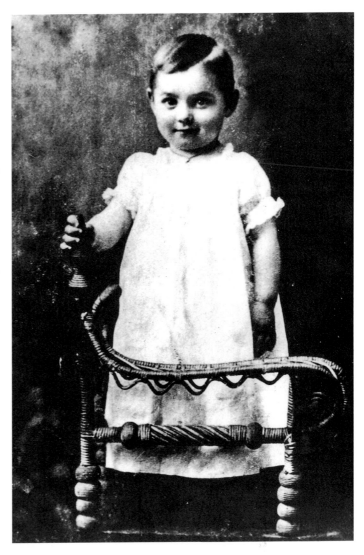

10 A toddler of 18 months, Clark is already posing with that dimpled smile that would later become famous (courtesy Harrison County Historical Society, Ohio).

a boom of its own then, with oil wells discovered on farms nearby drawing workers. Henry Dunlap and Mariah Frances Richards had five children, and before long Will had developed a close friendship with one of the daughters.

Although Jennie Dunlap was still living at home, she was no young girl. The manager of her own successful dressmaking and milliner business, the 32-year-old was a tall, slender, gentle, independent woman with a mind of her own and an immaculate dress sense to go along with her line of work. She could quickly make and be seen wearing the latest fashions first amongst the women of Hopedale.

Will, something of an independent businessman himself, was so taken with her that he soon proposed and they were married in April 1903 in Hopedale. Wanting his family to be complete again, Will promptly returned to Meadville for Clark, but the Hershelmans were reluctant to let Clark go away with a father he hardly knew. Clark didn't want to go either, so it was not without some tears that the family was reunited back in Hopedale.

However, Clark and his new mother quickly warmed to each other. In later life, he always remembered her fondly as a wonderful woman who knew just how to treat this boy who had not yet been able to experience the security and love of a complete family of his own. She was, he would say, a kind, affectionate and cultured mother who always treated him as if he had been her own.

11   Clark showed an early aptitude for the arts, and so Jennie and Will agreed to ensure that he have a good education. Jennie didn't want him working on oil rigs if she could help it. She read to him and encouraged him to read, and she taught him to sing and to play the piano. Will invested in the 72 volumes of the *Library of the World's Best Literature*, the complete works of Shakespeare and the 16-volume *History of the Bible*, and that love of books remained with Clark all his life. His house in Encino had a respectable library of leatherbound and book-plated volumes; actor Myrna Loy recalled that Clark loved literature so much he would read poetry to her during their breaks while they were working on *Parnell*.

11   Clark is photographed with his stepmother, Jennie Dunlap, c. 1910 (courtesy Harrison County Historical Society, Ohio).

12   While working in West Virginia during August 1903, Will Gable fell ill and had to return to the Dunlap house in Hopedale to recuperate for a month. While forced to rest, he no doubt had much time on his hands to think over the family circumstances and apparently decided it was about time his family had a place of their own. The next spring, he purchased some land on the outskirts of the town.

Seven years later, now settled, earning a steady income and with Clark in school, Will made his final payment on the large, gently sloping allotment fronting Mill Street and began building the family home into which the Gables finally moved in 1912. The spacious, two-story, L-shaped timber home looks much the same today as it did then with its gabled roof, wide front porch, and big bay window looking out over the sweep of the front yard down to the street.

12 **The Gable house in Hopedale as it looks today (courtesy the Gable Archive).**

It must have been a wonderful house for a small boy to be raised in, with space in which to run around and full of the rich smells of Jennie's cooking that would have drawn him into the kitchen to sit at the table where he could watch her and talk. His father would typically arrive home from work on a Saturday afternoon and proceed to try and get reacquainted with his wife and son. If he'd made enough money that week, Will would often be carrying some special treat for Clark. Once it was a bicycle; another time he had a pool table delivered that made Clark about the only boy in town to have one of his very own.

All in all, the Gables were the very image of a respectable, comfortably well-off, middle-class family. They were members of the local Methodist Church where they woud attend every Sunday morning. Clark had publicly converted during a revival when he was 12 and Will was the Sunday School superintendent.

13 When Clark was about ten, his mother must have figured she had taught him all she could and sent him off for formal music lessons. Clark chose as his preferred instrument a mellophone, or sliphorn, a type of French horn used in marching bands. He quickly became so good at blowing his horn that he was invited to join the Hopedale Brass Band by its director, John Kyle; he was the youngest person in the band. Clark would recall later how he swelled with pride when the audience applauded after his first performance and he was allowed to take his bow.

He was still playing in the band during the summer of 1914 when they presented outdoor Friday evening concerts for the townspeople on the high school campus, and during the following year when they presented a grand Independence Day concert.

13 The youngest member of the Hopedale Brass Band, Clark stands behind the drum proudly holding his mellophone, c. 1912 (courtesy Harrison County Historical Society, Ohio).

14 A confident, relaxed Clark taking up more than his share of space in his first year at Hopedale High (1915-16). (Clark is second from the right in the second row from the front, Thelma Lewis is second from right in the row behind him, and Tommy Lewis is next to Clark, third from right. George Dunlap, superintendent, is first on the left in the back row. Notice the prevalent young female fashion for big hair bows. Courtesy Harrison County Historical Society, Ohio.)

14 Should it be any surprise that Clark is the only boy in his row refusing to stand the same way as the rest? Can we see in that direct-gaze at the camera the beginning of an affinity with the lens? Looking at photographs like these, we find it tempting to seek the man within the child.

Clark had already been hanging around the Hopedale Primary School for some time before he was formally enrolled in 1907, and by the time he finished grade three he was giving the recitation in the closing exercises and singing solos and duets. In 1910 he moved on to Intermediate, grades four, five and six, where he completed sixth grade first in his class and was named a Scholarship Honor Pupil.

Clark was now a promising young man in the Hopedale community: a credit to his school, an active member of his church and a talented musician. In the fall of 1913 he entered the Hopedale Grammar School, a single class consisting of grades seven and eight, from which he graduated in May of 1915. This would be all the schooling that many of his friends would receive, but Jennie and Will Gable had bigger ambitions for their son.

So, in early September 1915, Clark enrolled as a freshman at Hopedale High School in the class group that you see above. There were three teachers, two of them doubling as principal and superintendent. It was a happy and successful year for him, during which he became firm friends with Tommy and his sister, the pretty, redheaded Thelma Lewis. Many years later

15 The Yale farm house as it looks today from Alliance Road (courtesy the Gable Archive).

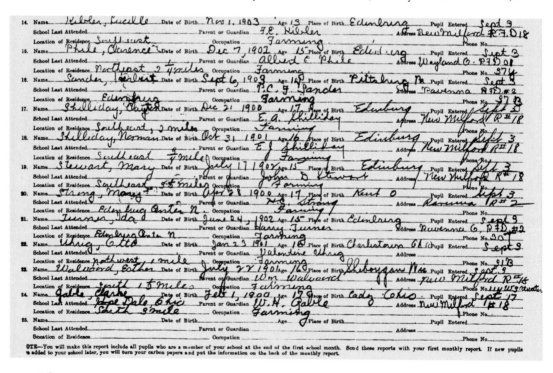

16 The Edinburg Centralized High School class register for 1917 showing Clark's enrollment at the bottom of the page as of September 17 (courtesy the Gable Archive).

Thelma would recall that Clark had been her first date, but at the time she hadn't thought him particularly good-looking, mainly because his ears were too large.

Marjorie Miller, a pretty girl two years younger, also later claimed to be his childhood sweetheart. Clark seems to have started a trend early.

15 Casting around for a more stable income, Will decided he'd return to his family roots and move the family north to a farm not far from Akron. The Gables sold their Hopedale property in August of 1917 for $2900 and a few weeks later purchased the Ensinger farm some 70 miles northeast at Yale, or New Milford as it was known then, near Ravenna. As often happens, Clark found it difficult to cope with this sudden change. He didn't get along with the local kids very well; he was taller and bigger and preferred to ride a horse to school. So he kept in touch with his friends from back home and they visited each other periodically.

Yale was a rural area rather than a population center, the nearest of which was the town of Ravenna a few miles away. The Gables' new home was just another farm out there by the side of a long road, and like any other farm boy in that rural area Clark was expected to be out of bed early in the morning to help his father with feeding the hogs, the chickens and other livestock, with ploughing, forking hay, fencing and all those other chores that keep a farm running. Eventually it became too claustrophobic for a young man who felt that life had a lot more to offer. By 1918, Clark had decided to join his friend Andy Means in the bright lights of Akron.

16–17 As you can see by the register, Edinburg High was a small school. It was about three miles down the road from the Gable farm with a total enrollment of 24 students in grades nine, ten and eleven. There were 14 boys and 10 girls with an age range between 13

17 A page from the Edinburg Centralized High School class record showing Clark's eleventh grade report for October 1917 (courtesy the Gable Archive).

and 17. Clark's age is listed as 17 because his birth year is written as 1900; he was actually a year younger. The number of families that have listed their occupation as "farming" gives an indication of the rural nature of the area. The two-story Edinburg brick schoolhouse was quite new and modern for its time, replacing an earlier structure destroyed by fire. It would eventually be demolished and replaced by the current South-East High School.

Although not happy at school, Clark was certainly no truant and displays an excellent series of grades with an average of 81. A man who would later be noted for his contribution to the arts, Clark here shows highest scores for his agriculture and physics subjects.

18–19   About the time he moved to Akron, Clark met Charles Smith, who came from that same area. Ukuleles were a popular musical instrument in the early 20th century. Because of their size, they were portable and their basic stringing meant they were easy for anyone to play, especially someone with musical training like Clark. It's no surprise, then, to see

Clark and Charles entertaining themselves one sunny morning with a uke along with some spoon percussion on the porch of the house where Clark lived. By the look of those shined shoes, creased pants and collars and ties, it was probably a Sunday morning. Given that both these boys were 18 or 19, you can get an idea of how big Clark was at this age by comparing not only his height with that of Charles but also the size of his hands.

Smith would later meet the woman who became his wife in Meadville. His grandson Thomas says it's a family legend that they met while Charles was there with Clark during one of his periodic visits with relatives.

20–21   Rubber became the sticky lifeblood of Akron, Ohio, after Benjamin Goodrich set up his factory there in 1871 to take advantage of railroad and canal junctions. With the rapid development of the automobile industry come the 20th century, fol-

18   Clark (left) and his friend Charles Smith forming a musical duo on the front porch of a house where Clark was boarding in Akron (with permission Thomas P. Smith).

lowed by the onset of World War I, the need for rubber goods boomed and between 1910 and 1920 the city's population soared from 69,000 to 208,000, the greatest population growth of any American city during that period. People were attracted to Akron's labor force from neighboring rural areas like iron filings to a magnet. Goodyear alone employed 30,000 people, and a good worker could earn five to seven dollars for an eight-hour shift (good money in those days) after a month's experience.

Akron became known as the rubber capital of the world, home to the plants of the Miller, Goodyear and Firestone companies, and Clark wanted to be right there in the middle of it. After much heated argument with his father, who with some wisdom could see this was a boom that one day would bust and that there was more security

19 Clark (middle) and his friends Charles Smith (left) and Ray Hoobler pose very formally in front of a military backdrop in an Akron photographer's studio (with permission Thomas P. Smith).

20 Clark at far left, probably about age 17, with fellow workers in the powerhouse at Miller Tire and Rubber, Akron, Ohio (courtesy the Gable Archive).

21 A well-dressed Clark, looking every inch the prosperous office worker in Akron (with permission Thomas P. Smith).

on the land, Clark finally left for Akron and his friend Andy Means when he was 17.

He found accommodation in Akron and began work as a clerk in the timekeeping office at the Firestone rim plant. The following year, unable to persuade Firestone to give him a raise, he took on the same work at the Miller Tire and Rubber Company where his charming personality and big smile, readily recognizable under that cap, made him popular.

In 1920, however, his newfound prosperous independence was shaken by the untimely death of his stepmother followed by that very bust in rubber production his father had foreseen. Clark was reduced to selling shirts and ties at Gates and Kittle's haberdashery, and to working at Haun's drugstore. Unable to manage an entire farm alone, his father eventually sold it, returning to the occupation he knew best. Will headed south to the new oil boom in Oklahoma, but not before visiting with his son in Akron (where they posed for that portrait seen earlier).

Acting Life

22–23   One night while Clark was working in the Miller Tire factory in Akron and boarding with Lewis and Emily Grether at 24 Steiner Avenue, he had an opportunity to go to a theater performance. Sitting there in the dark he had an epiphany.

The Ed Clark Lilley–Pauline McLean Players had arrived in town to perform a season of Richard Walton Tully's *The Bird of Paradise* at the 2,000-seat Music Hall, sometimes known as the German-American Hall, which stood downtown on East Exchange Street. Opened on September 15, 1904, with a concert by the Victor Herbert Orchestra, the Hall's cost of some $65,000 had been financed by German-American multi-millionaire Paul Werner. The hall had an enormous dining room that could seat 800 and a stage expansive enough to accommodate opera performances; Werner intended it as a focus for activities for the German immigrants who had settled in the area. But its name, if not its audience, was changed by the wave of anti–German sentiment that swept through the country during World War I. The elaborate, towered brick hall would be demolished in 1929 to make way for the home of the *Akron Times-Press* newspaper which in 1938 became the *Akron Beacon-Journal*.

The Bird of Paradise was a romantic melodrama about an Hawaiian princess who commits suicide by leaping into a volcano because of her unrequited love for a handsome American. It was often the custom for traveling shows to hire bit players and extras from the local population; when one of Clark's work colleagues, Eddie Grisdale, was offered a job, he handed in his notice at the factory. Unhappy with his final payslip, Eddie had asked Clark to check it for him. Clark found an error in Eddie's favor and his grateful friend had rewarded him with a ticket to the show. So when the lights went up that night, there was Clark. The show featured tropical atmosphere, beautiful music and seductive dancers. He was absolutely entranced. Perhaps he heard echoes of school plays and band concerts in Hopedale or perhaps he saw a means of escaping a future of factories and oil rigs. Either way, he left that theater walking a different path in his life.

From then on, Ed Lilley and his wife Pauline MacLean couldn't get rid of him. Clark haunted the stage door and took to eating in the same diner as the actors. He would run errands, act as an unpaid call boy, sweep the stage, *anything* to be able to stay on and soak up the atmosphere and learn the craft. In the end, Lilley let Clark walk on stage during a performance one night as a spear-carrier. He didn't fall on his face and as far as Clark was concerned, even though Lilley couldn't remember him later from among the hundreds who'd been hired in various places, his future was assured.

"CAPTAIN RACKET"

—o—

A Comedy to be Given by Hopedale High School, in Patton's Hall, Hopedale, March 11.

—o—

CAST:

Captain Robert Racket, part time lawyer, whole time liar,
                                                    Andrew Means
Obadiah Dawson, his uncle, from Japan . . . . . . Thomas Lewis
Timothy Tolman, his friend, married for money . . . Clarke Gable
Mr. Dalroy, his father-in-law . . . .⎫
Hobson, waiter . . . .⎬ Wilson Hoobler
Clarice, Captain's pretty wife, out for a lark . . . Virginia Hervey
Mrs. Tolman, a lady of temper . . . . Eva Skeeles
Katy, a mischievous maid . . . . Eileen Bell
Tootsy, the kid, Tim's olive branch.

—o—

SYNOPSIS:

Act I. Place, Tim's country home on the Hudson. Time, a morning in September. Tim removes a sliver. "A dove or an old hen." Tim never had a chance. Bob receives a letter. The Captain's fancy takes flight and trouble begins. The theatre and Cafe Gloriana.

Act II. Place, the same. Time, next morning. How one yarn requires another. Tim a dead man. A bill for damages. The two lunatics meet. "The greatest liar unhung." Now the trouble increases and the Captain prepares for war.

Act III. Place, the same. Time, evening of the same day. More misery. A general muddle. "Dance or you'll die." Cornered at last. The Captain owns up. All serene.

Time of playing two hours.

22 A program advertising Clark's first known appearance on stage, as Timothy Tolman in the Hopedale High School's production of *Captain Racket* on March 11, 1916 (courtesy Harrison County Historical Society, Ohio).

23 The Akron Music Hall, originally known as the German-American Hall or simply the Deutsches Haus, where Clark saw his first major theater production (courtesy Akron-Summit County Public Library, Ohio).

But it wouldn't be as simple as that; it rarely is. After Clark's stepmother died, everything changed. He no longer had his factory job and then both his father and the theater troupe left town. Clark was left with little choice but to join him working on Oklahoma oil rigs. But then an uncle's trust fund came due when Clark turned 21. He returned to Meadville to collect the money, then caught a train to Kansas City where he heard that traveling tent shows were hiring. Clark's tent show career only lasted a few weeks until his particular show was trapped by snow in Butte, Montana.

Broke and hungry, Clark piled green logs for a lumber mill until he had enough money to get to Portland, Oregon, where he found a job modeling neckties at Meir and Frank's department store. He soon found he had much to talk about with another young man there, Earle Larimore, who was descended from a long line of theater people and who would later become a distinguished actor himself. His aunt was actor Laura Hope Crews, whom Clark would meet many years later as *Gone with the Wind*'s Aunt Pittypat. Earle was then starring in a production with his Red Lantern Players. When Earle was offered the chance to direct the Astoria Players Stock Company by their manager Rex Jewell, Clark tagged along to the auditions.

There he met the elfin beauty Franz Dorfler, who was also auditioning. Before long they

24   The stern-wheeler *Bailey Gatzert*, a typical example of the riverboat on which the Astoria Players would have sailed down the Columbia River (courtesy Pacific County Historical Society).

were hopelessly in love and on their way down the Columbia River with the Astoria Players in the summer of 1922.

24   For many years, legend has credited the *Bailey Gatzert* with being the actual riverboat on board which the Players embarked for Astoria, but actually she was no longer sailing the Columbia River by then. Nevertheless, she was a typical example of the type of craft that plied this majestic river until superseded by railroads and automobiles not long after Clark and Franz set sail with the Astoria Players.

Clark was the only man Franz Dorfler ever loved, yet she never saw him in any of his movies because it hurt too much. His gestures, his smile, his dimples remained those of the man she'd very nearly married. Barely over five feet in height with bright eyes, an engaging smile and her hair in a fashionably short bob, Frances Doerfler was raised on a farm at Silverton, Oregon. She always wanted to be on the stage and left home for the footlights of Portland as soon as possible, altering her name to Franz Dorfler while gaining experience with walk-on parts and chorus lines.

The Astoria Players auditions were her big chance to try out for a major speaking role, and there it was that Cupid's arrow hit home. Clark was smitten the first time he saw her and within a few days had swept her off her feet with professions of undying devotion. Rex Jewell, on the other hand, remained unconvinced that the clumsy Clark had an acting bone in his body and refused to sign him up. Threatened with separation, the panicked young lovers laid siege to Jewell's office until the beleaguered manager agreed to hire them both. So they departed with the Players down the Columbia on a riverboat to Astoria.

By the time they all arrived back in Portland at the end of October, no richer in money but wealthier in experience, Clark and Franz had publicly announced their engagement. So, the couple then spent a few weeks at the Doerfler farm while the family got to know their potential son-in-law. Clark hoped to marry soon, but a cautious Franz wanted them to be better established before taking such a big step. Consequently, she returned to Portland for further music study and Clark went to work stacking and loading lumber at the Silver Falls Timber Company in Silverton on forty cents a day.

Before long, Franz was offered a job in a new theater company touring the Northwest, and then early the following year it was Clark's turn to move to Portland for music study and work. He was so successful at both that a proud Franz agreed to marry him when she returned from Seattle at the end of the year. But Fate was now weaving a different pattern, and Franz made the mistake of encouraging Clark to take lessons from the well-known actress and drama coach Josephine Dillon. None of their lives was ever the same again. At year's end, Clark called off the engagement to focus on studying for the stage. Franz was shattered, refusing to eat and unable to sleep for days.

They met again in San Francisco in 1925, when Clark was appearing there in *What Price Glory?* Over the next few years they stayed in touch intermittently as Franz moved to Los Angeles in 1930, but drifted apart after Clark married Ria. Twelve years later Franz appeared as a witness for Clark in the Violet Norton paternity trial; a grateful (or conscience-stricken) Clark found her a little work at MGM, but he never saw her again. Even at eighty, tears would still well in Franz's eyes at the mention of his name.

The *Bailey Gatzert*, or the "Daily Bastard" as she was sometimes called by riverboat men who didn't appreciate her broad wake, was one of the most famous of the Columbia River steamboats that plied between Portland and Astoria. Constructed in the John Holland shipyards at Ballard, Washington, in 1890 and named after a prominent retail businessman who was the first and only Jewish mayor of Seattle, the *Bailey* was a luxuriously appointed 177-foot-long, 32-foot-wide sternwheeler designed for passenger runs and excursions. Beginning operations on the Seattle to Tacoma and Olympia run, often in competition with the side-wheeler *T. J. Potter*, she was transferred to the Columbia River by the White Collar Line in 1892 on the run between Portland and Astoria. She became renowned for her speed and elegance, demonstrated in many a steamboat race. Purchased by the Dalles, Portland & Astoria Navigation Company (the Regulator Line) in 1904, she became so popular during the 1905 Lewis and Clark Exposition while making twice-daily round trips from Portland to the Cascade Canal and Locks that the *Bailey Gatzert March* was composed by Decker and Velguth in her honor.

However, in time the *Bailey* succumbed to the automobile quite literally. Despite being rebuilt to 194 feet long, she returned to Puget Sound in 1918 to eventually suffer the indignity of being converted to a 25-vehicle automobile ferry, after which she became a floating machine shop on Seattle's Lake Union.

The *Bailey Gatzert*'s important contribution to history was finally recognized when she was depicted on a U.S. postage stamp in 1996. Today her name-board, seven-foot-diameter pilot wheel, whistle, pilot house bell and company flag, along with a model of the sternwheeler, can be seen on display at the Columbia Gorge Interpretive Center Museum in Stevenson, Washington.

25   Old Cinderville, as Astoria was sometimes known for good reason, had been first settled as Fort Astoria (on the south bank of the Columbia River where it met the sea) by a party of John Jacob Astor's fur trappers in 1811. Promptly claimed by the British, it wasn't handed to America until 1818 whereupon it burned down for the first time. The rebuilt fur-trading town was immortalized by Washington Irving in 1836 in his biographical account *Astoria* and it never looked back, becoming in time a bustling deep-water port and gateway to the Columbia River. By 1922, it had reached a peak population of 15,000 people who worked predominantly in the fishing and lumber industries.

At that time a Scotsman by the name of Kirk McKean owned the local Astoria Theatre. Reading about Earl Larimore's success in Portland with the Red Lantern Players, he had been inspired to try and improve local culture somewhat and so he'd formed the Astoria Players Stock Company, hiring Rex Jewell as manager and Larimore as director.

So, on the night of July 15, 1922, the Astoria Theatre curtain went up before a crowd of 350 on the Players' opening performance of the three-act comedy-drama *It Can't Be Done*. The play was doing well, with everyone laughing in all the right places, until midway through the second act when the lights went out. The audience soon became restive, and some booing and hissing began. McKean went on stage holding a candle and calmed the audience by singing some Scottish songs. Then some of the cast filled in with a little vaudeville until the frantic backstage crew had the lights working again and the show went on.

25   The plaque on the corner of 12th Street and Exchange in Astoria to mark the site of the Astoria Theatre, where Clark had his first adult credited speaking role on stage (with permission from Sheryl Todd).

Over the next few days McKean began to hear rumors that the blackout might well have been a hint from Astoria Light and Power concerning some outstanding bills of his business partner, Joseph Kelley. Shortly after, Kelley abruptly left town with all the money. From then on, the Players had to be paid with equal shares from each performance's takings. One of the actors who didn't like the new conditions decided to return to Portland, and suddenly Clark "Billy" Gable had his first regular acting job.

On Wednesday night, July 19, 1922, the Players presented popular one-act plays rewritten by Jewel as *Bits of Life*. The first act was the farce *Are You a Mason?* in which Clark just had a walk-on part but in the second, *Dregs*, he had an actual speaking role as a detective. For the first time as an adult, Clark Gable's voice was heard on stage. For the third act, a send-up of the old melodrama *The Villain Still Pursued Her*, Clark was Billy Dresssuitcase — a baby! As the biggest baby that audience had surely ever

26 A close-up portrait of Clark in the role of Sergeant Quirt in the May 1925 Los Angeles production of What Price Glory? (courtesy the Gable Archive).

seen, he brought the house down. The following Sunday and Monday, Clark was the cook Eliza Goober in *When Women Rule*, starring Earle's sweetheart Peggy Martin as the first woman mayor of Astoria, and on the Thursday they began a run of the well-known play *Corinne of the Circus*.

By now, though, Astoria seemed to be tiring of culture. Audience numbers started to fall off for the group's run of *Blundering Billy*, in which Clark played an old sea captain, and the Players were soon rationing food, even begging for salmon at the docks. When they shared out their takings on Wednesday, August 2, after their performance of *Mr. Bob* they each held only $1.30 in their hands. The dream was over, but they couldn't even muster enough money to pay for the trip back up the river.

Undaunted, the resourceful Rex Jewell went to work locating venues and they played *Corinne of the Circus* from small town to logging camp upstream to Portland, living off their door takings, eating some days and not others, sometimes sleeping around a campfire or on the deck of whatever craft would carry them on the river.

Only a few months after the players left town, another huge fire that burned for 10 hours wiped out 30 blocks of downtown Astoria including the Astoria Theatre. It was replaced by the Liberty Theatre in a different location, and within a few years no one remembered that the town and its original theater had figured so importantly in the life of one of Hollywood's major movie stars. Former local historian, consultant to Steven Spielberg, vintage car owner and charity food deliverer Abel Olson and his wife Marian never forgot, though, and they financed the placement of a plaque that today marks the site where Clark Gable's acting career really began.

26 Hollywood in 1924 was a town where thousands of people wanted to make it in the movies just as much as Mr. Clark Gable did. Thirty-five hundred people were known to turn up to a casting call for 35. In the process of developing his acting method in Portland with Josephine Dillon as his coach, Clark had also developed a personal relationship with Josephine that became close enough for them to leave Oregon together for Los Angeles. Josephine was convinced that Clark could become a major actor if only he worked hard enough, and work him she did. Five months after they arrived, when he was 23 and she was in the vicinity of 40, they married.

Clark was lucky to find some walk-on movie roles while Josephine continued to train him. Tiring of the fruitless search for meatier roles, Clark eventually fell back to where he knew he would be treated seriously — the stage. Clark heard that the husband-and-wife team of Louis O. Macloon and Lillian Albertson's West Coast Road Company was holding auditions for *Romeo and Juliet*. Unbeknownst to Clark, they were in desperate need of some tall broad-shouldered soldiers, so when he came walking down the aisle that day he was hired on the spot, before he had a chance to read a line. For the next six years he would continue to work under Albertson's direction so, while Dillon might have taught him the theory of it all, Lillian Albertson's impact on the development of Clark's acting technique should never be ignored. When the actor playing Mercutio left a week after they opened, Clark was given a chance to appear in his place. Albertson worked with him night after night trying to refine his stage coordination and movement, despairing one day whether anyone had ever seen an actor who walked more like a truck driver than Clark Gable.

Still, Albertson must have thought something was working by the time she cast him in his first major character role on stage, as Private Kiper in her West Coast production of the popular Broadway play *What Price Glory?* Justifying her intuition, Clark was so good that she quickly re-cast him in one of the two male lead roles (Sergeant Quirt) not long after the play opened in Los Angeles. The play had been written by Maxwell Anderson and Laurence Stallings, a former World War I Marine captain who had lost a leg at Belleau Wood. Opening in Broadway at the 1000-seat Plymouth Theatre in early September 1924, it had been both wildly popular and immediately embroiled in controversy. While theater critics hailed it as the most credible and realistic play about war then seen, many in the audience were offended by the explicit and gritty vocabulary and the play's realistic, non-heroic treatment of World War I soldiers at the front. When the men aren't chasing Germans they're chasing pretty local girls, one of whom becomes pregnant; they are nevertheless happy to abandon her as they leave for the front. The controversy didn't end when the play was made into a silent movie directed by Raoul Walsh in 1926; lip-readers amongst the audiences were quick to complain about the level of profanity being uttered by the actors (none of which appeared on the intertitle cards of course). A much more successful film version of the play, known as *The Big Parade*, had already been made by King Vidor the year before with a screenplay written by Stallings himself.

Not in any small part due to all this publicity, *What Price Glory?* ran for over 400 performances in New York, and it did very well on the other side of the country as well. Clark remained in his co-starring role for another 15 weeks, so acclaimed that he continued to reprise that role as the production traveled to San Francisco in June, then to Portland, Seattle, Vancouver and back to Los Angeles. Over the next two years Clark would appear in seven more plays for the Macloons: *Lullaby, The Copperhead, Lady Frederick, Madam X, Lucky Sam McCarver,* and *Chicago*.

27   Because of passing time and lost records, the order of Clark's first silent movie roles has to be assessed these days by release dates. According to this system, Clark's first confirmed appearances on screen are as Lady Andrea Pellor's brother in B.P. Schulberg's *White Man* (November 1, 1924), followed by a walk-on as a soldier in the guard during Ernst Lubitsch's *Forbidden Paradise* (November 30, 1924), and then as an extra in Wesley Ruggles' *The Pacemakers* (March 1, 1925). However, he is also reputed to appear in uncredited walk-ons in Denison Clift's *The Great Diamond Mystery* (October 5, 1924), and in Malcolm St. Clair's *Fighting Blood* (November 23, 1924).

The Pacemakers was actually a series of 12 complete two-reel comedies, and each title was a play on a popular film: *Welcome Granger* (*Welcome Stranger*), *The Great Decide* (*The Great Divide*), *The Covered Flagon* (*The Covered Wagon*), and *What Price Gloria?* (*What Price Glory?*). They were directed by Wesley Ruggles, who would be nominated for an Academy Award for his direction of *Cimarron* (1931). He'd begun as an actor himself in 1915 before moving quickly to director, and *The Pacemakers* was already his 23rd film in eight years. In 1942 one of his last movies would be with a more well-known Clark Gable: *Somewhere I'll Find You*.

Clark's role in *The Pacemakers* was followed by three more recognizable silent roles. In August 1925, he appeared as an uncredited soldier and ballroom extra along with an equally young and uncredited Joan Crawford in Erich von Stroheim's *The Merry Widow*, and then in October he could be seen in an uncredited walk-on as a college athlete in another Ruggles film, *The Plastic Age*, which proved to be the film that brought fame to the "It" girl, Clara

27   Clark as an extra, standing third from the right at the rear, in *The Pacemakers* (1925) (courtesy the Gable Archive).

Bow. Clark wasn't the only uncredited face in this film who later became famous: Janet Gaynor and Carole Lombard both appeared in bit parts as co-eds.

In December 1925, Clark appeared in a small role as Archie West in Paul Powell's *North Star* with a dog named Strongheart. Powell is barely remembered now, but he was a pioneer writer-director who made over 80 films during a 16-year career, including the original versions of *Pollyanna* (1920) starring Mary Pickford and *Black Narcissus* (1929), famously remade in 1947 by Michael Powell starring Deborah Kerr. Although Clark's roles may have seemed minor to the impatient budding star, they would all prove to be valuable training for him. In any case, if he thought working in the movies was a tough life at the moment, he was doing better than the young Gary Cooper who was still uncredited in *North Star* after two years in Hollywood and 13 movies!

There are rumors of Clark in other uncredited roles: as an extra in *Declassee* (April 1925), as a crowd extra along with about every other breathing actor in Hollywood in the silent version of *Ben-Hur* (December 1925), as an extra standing at a saloon bar in *The Johnstown Flood* (February 1926), as an extra in *One Minute to Play* (September 1926), and as an extra in Norma Talmadge's last talkie, *Du Barry, Woman of Passion* (October 1930).

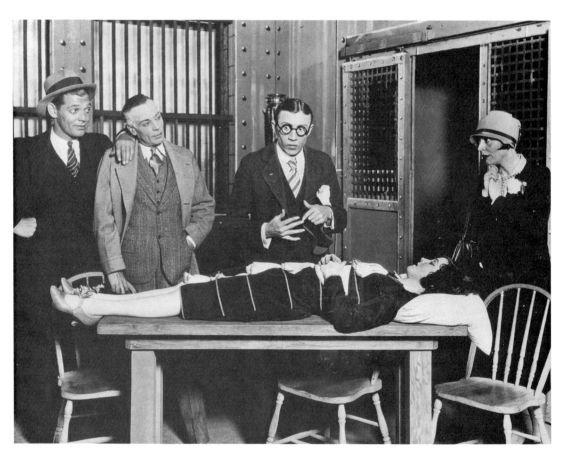

28   On stage at the Hollywood Music Box Theatre in Los Angeles in March 1927, Clark appears in Maureen Dallas Watkins' play *Chicago* as Jake, the reporter, on the left of this photograph. Next to him are Barry Townly, Paul Fix and Kay Campbell with Nancy Carroll on the table (courtesy the Gable Archive).

28   Despite those small roles, or perhaps because of them, Clark was unconvinced he had a future in movies and returned to work on the theater stage. In March of 1927 he appeared as Jake, the reporter, in the Los Angeles production of newspaperwoman Maureen Dallas Watkins' bitingly satiric play *Chicago*, once again under the direction of Lillian Albertson. Clark proceeded to turn a relatively minor role into one that gained him critical notice by giving his character some individual touches such as wearing his hat back on his head and adopting a characteristic stride. Nancy Carroll, who played Roxie Hart, always felt that Clark was the first actor to adopt what later became the stereotypical reporter "look" on stage and in film.

Audiences have been seeing *Chicago* in one form or another ever since. Cecil B. DeMille produced a silent film version the same year starring Phyllis Haver as Roxie; a 1942 remake, *Roxie Hart*, starred Ginger Rogers and Adolphe Menjou as the lawyer. The *Chicago* in which Clark appeared was the original play from which sprang the Broadway musical that opened in June 1975. The music was composed by John Kander with lyrics by Fred Ebb and choreography by John Fosse. That musical was in turn adapted for the 2002 film starring Rene Zellweger, Catherine Zeta-Jones and Richard Gere.

Maureen Dallas Watkins based *Chicago* on the columns she wrote for the *Chicago Tribune* while covering the 1924 trials of murderesses Beulah Annan and Belva Gaertner. Her original play satirized the rise of the celebrity criminal within a corrupt and media-hungry justice system. The lawyer of murderess Roxie Hart is so able to manipulate the press and the jury that not only is Roxie acquitted of her lover's murder but she becomes famous in the process. Likewise Beulah Annan, the model for Roxie Hart, became a media celebrity of the time when she was accused and then found not guilty of the murder of her lover Harry Kalstedt in her and her husband's bedroom in 1924. The character of Velma is based on Belva Gaertner, a cabaret singer in whose car the body of Walter Law was found. Two policemen testified they saw a woman get into the car and then they heard shots but Gaertner, too, was acquitted. William O'Brien, Annan's lawyer, and Gaertner's lawyer were melded by Watkins into the character of Billy Flynn.

A disillusioned Watkins left the *Tribune* after the trials and returned to Yale, where she had been studying previously, and there she wrote *Chicago* as an assignment for a playwriting course. Produced by Sam H. Harris and directed by George Abbott, the play became so popular at the Music Box Theatre on Broadway after its opening on December 30, 1926, that it ran for 172 performances. Gaertner was said to have been in the opening night audience.

Impressed by the play's success, Louis O. Macloon outbid a number of rival producers at the beginning of 1927 to buy the West Coast rights in order to stage the first performance of the play outside of New York. He had already signed a long-term lease on the Hollywood Music Box Theatre, and in early March he announced that *Chicago* would be opening there on the 22nd. Already appearing in a revue at the Music Box, 24-year-old Nancy Carroll was selected to play Roxie Hart, a role that ensured her future career. Clark was confirmed as reporter Jake, while his friend Paul Fix would be Amos. The same age as Clark, Fix would appear during his life in over 300 movies but was perhaps best known as Marshal Micah Torrance in the television series *The Rifleman*. Barry Townly, who played the cynical, spellbinding lawyer Billy Flynn, was a child actor and successful playwright who was also something of an adventurer, having just returned from a caravan expedition through the deserts of Libya where he lived with the Bedouin.

Before long, *Chicago* was being acclaimed as the best of that year's local theater season. Its run only ended in late May because, Macloon claimed, he had other booking commitments. The production toured to San Francisco where it played with equal success at the Lurie through July and August before Carroll had to return to Los Angeles and the Music Box for another

Macloon production, *Hit the Deck*. Clark was complemented by critics on the realism of his performance as the reporter and generously replied that his success was largely due to Albertson and Macloon's faith in him and to Lionel Barrymore, who had once advised him to never play a part straight but always to find some bit of individual character with which to imbue it.

29   The 980-seat Hollywood Music Box Theatre was practically new when Clark performed there, having opened on October 20, 1926. Designed by noted theater architects Octavius Morgan, J.A. Walls and Stiles O. Clements in Spanish Colonial style, the theater is still standing despite having passed through a number of incarnations since then. Initially used for staging elaborate Ziegfeld Follies–type musical revues, the theater was designed with an open-air cabaret space above the lobby. After some years as a live theater venue, it became the home *of Lux Radio Theatre* from 1936 to 1938 when major Hollywood stars could frequently be heard across the country reprising their film roles in cut-down live-to-air dramas. In all likelihood, Clark found himself back on that familiar stage during a broadcast.

After another period as a live theater in the early forties, the building became the Guild Theatre in 1945, remodeled and converted to film exhibition by Fox West Coast before being re-named the Fox Theatre. By the mid–1950s it was the Pix Theatre; on the new marquee, a spectacular neon display and vertical sign was mounted. The premiere of *Jaws* was held here in 1975 and of *Rocky* in 1976. But changing times threw some killer punches, and after the theater closed in 1977 it sat empty for years. Fortunately, unlike many other theatres, this one wasn't eventually demolished but re-opened again for live theater in March 1985 as the Henry Fonda Theatre, becoming the home for a number of Broadway productions (such as *Lend Me*

29   The exterior of the Hollywood Music Box Theatre as it looks today at 6126 Hollywood Boulevard. The original Spanish colonial façade is still there behind the cladding and eventually it will be restored (photographer: Bill Counter, http://www.losangelestheatres.blogspot.com).

a Tenor and *Nunsense*) and for various concerts by well-known artists.

In June 2002, it was renamed the Music Box @ Fonda and a restoration program was initiated that has since revealed many of the original architectural features. The former open-air cabaret room is once again entertaining customers as a reception area while the theater space now hosts a variety of special entertainment events.

30   In the summer of 1928, Clark arrived in New York after a long season with Gene Lewis' stock company in Houston, Texas. He signed with the major Chamberlain Brown agency and plunged into four weeks of rehearsal for *Machinal* with co-star Zita Johann, opening at the Plymouth Theatre on September 7, 1928. Although *Machinal* played the full three-month season to critical acclaim, for the next eighteen months Clark drifted through a number of theater productions between Philadelphia, Atlantic City and New York City with varying degrees of success. Among them was the three-act Howard Irving Young drama *Hawk Island*, which opened at New York's

30   Menacing the audience from behind bars, Clark is seen here in his role of "Killer" Mears, the leader of the prisoner revolt in the 1930 Los Angeles production of *The Last Mile* (courtesy the Gable Archive).

Longacre Theatre on September 16, 1929. Critics thought that Clark handled his lead role well. The play still closed after only 24 performances despite being directed by Young himself. Perhaps someone should have noticed there were thirteen in the cast. After that, Clark couldn't find a steady job until March 1930, when he was finally given a good part in *Love, Honor and Betray* at the Eltinge Theatre. Then Clark heard again from his old friend Lillian Albertson.

Maintaining her strong faith in Clark's potential, Albertson offered him the lead in *The Last Mile*, which she and her husband Louis Macloon wanted to take to the West Coast. With a title referring to the last walk of a condemned prisoner, this was a disturbing play about a group of death-row inmates who figure they have nothing to lose and attempt a last-minute break-out after one of them is executed. When the escape fails, they take hostages and barricade themselves in while the police lay siege and attempt to blast their way into the prison with dynamite. With Spencer Tracy playing Mears, it was already a hit on Broadway and regarded as a powerful indictment of capital punishment.

Clark went to see the play and thought Tracy so impressive in the role that he'd never be able to do it justice. Doubts about his ability to play certain roles assailed Clark a number of times during his career, but usually the role would end up being a star vehicle for him. Clark was notoriously conservative when it came to work and his money, and it often took much persuasion by studio bosses, agents, wives and friends for him to venture into unknown character territory.

This role was no exception, and it wasn't until just four weeks before the projected opening date that Clark reluctantly accepted Albertson's offer and arrived in Los Angeles. Rehearsals began immediately behind locked doors at the Majestic Theatre, where *The Last Mile* opened on June 2, 1930. It took the town by storm, quickly becoming the fashionably controversial play that one just had to see. Clark was acclaimed in a role in which he became part-man, part-animal caged in his cell, pacing it, gripping the bars in his huge hands as if he would pry them apart and leap into the audience. The harsh top-lighting cut deep shadows on his face as his voice snarled in deep hatred at his fate. The critics loved both the play and Clark Gable in it, and audiences packed the theater night after night.

Amongst them was actor-director Lionel Barrymore who had previously worked with Clark on stage and so probably realized more than most people just how far he had come. Lionel eventually persuaded Clark to do a screen test for him followed by another for director Mervyn LeRoy. Although Clark was unsuccessful in those, agent Ruth Collier was in the screening audience and saw something in Clark that others didn't. She signed him immediately, and assigned her assistant Minna Wallis, sister of producer-director Hal B. Wallis, to him. Minna found him a part in a Pathé Western called *The Painted Desert* at $750 a week, and Clark Gable's career in film had begun.

31   Remarkably, with the exception of Edwards who doesn't appear to have done military service, the men in this photo taken during the making of a movie that showcased the technology of war would all eventually be involved in World War II and survive.

Hell Divers was produced and directed by George W. Hill and shot in late 1931. It was the last of 12 movies that Gable made that year, predominantly without his yet-to-be-famous moustache, and not one of his most successful. There had been too much recent competition within this genre and, besides, it was not a strongly plot-driven movie. The original story was by Lt. Comdr. Frank W. "Spig" Wead U.S.N.R., who had commanded a fighter squadron before becoming paralyzed as the result of a fall, but the screenplay was worked on by at least six people and looked like it. Cinematographer Charles Marshall, an ex-air service flight instructor whose acclaimed aerial work can be seen in such films as *The Flying Fleet* (1929), *Captains of the Clouds* (1942) and *God Is My Co-Pilot* (1945), was in charge of the aerial photography; he would work again with Clark in 1933 on *Night Flight*. A clip from *Hell Divers* can be seen in the 1957 film about "Spig" Wead's life, *The Wings of Eagles* with John Wayne.

Hell Divers takes its name from the nickname of the Curtiss F8C "Helldivers" biplane dive bombers that feature in it, and it contains much actual footage shot aboard the early aircraft carrier *Saratoga*, converted from a battlecruiser hull and later sunk as a test ship at Bikini Atoll in 1946. Shooting footage on aircraft carriers only dated back to 1929 and *The Flying Fleet*, another Wead story shot on board the U.S.S. *Langley*, so it was quite a feat for those days. The Naval Air Station at North Island, California, was the major exterior land location.

Gable and Beery never got along well off-screen, and much of the scripting of them for this film as competing chief petty officer air gunners took advantage of their touchy attitudes towards each other. The movie is never so much about them, however, as about glorifying new naval technology such as the world's largest aircraft carrier at that time, naval airships and advances in new techniques such as dive bombing. Rather ironically, this film became well-known to Japanese bomber pilots and the efficiency of the techniques demonstrated in it would come back to haunt the U.S. Navy at Pearl Harbor.

The man on the left of this photo is Cliff Edwards (1895–1971), who with Clark is one of the only two people in this group who never piloted an aircraft. Instead, Edwards gained fame for a different form of flight: He would be the voice of Jiminy Cricket in Disney's *Pinoc-*

31 Standing by a Curtiss F8C-4 aircraft of Fighting Squadron 1-B at Naval Air Station, North Island, California, on September 16, 1931, while filming *Hell Divers* are (left to right) Cliff Edwards, Lt. (Jnr.) John S. Thach U.S.N., Clark Gable, Wallace Beery, Lt. (Jnr.) H.S. Duckworth U.S.N., and Lt. (Jnr.) E.P. Southwick U.S.N. (courtesy Naval History and Heritage Command).

chio (1940), a role which he repeated many times and which was his last film role in 1970. Edwards was originally well-known onstage in clubs and vaudeville during the 1920s as the hit ukulele jazz virtuoso and singer "Ukulele Ike." It was while playing at the Los Angeles Orpheum that he caught the attention of producer Irving Thalberg and thus MGM, appearing in Buster Keaton comedies and in a number of Westerns before moving to Disney and to national radio and television. However, fame did not appear to do Edwards any favors; he battled with bankruptcy, alcoholism and drug problems for most of his life and died a pauper. The Actors Fund of America and the Motion Picture and Television Fund paid for his burial and Disney paid for his grave marker at the Pierce Brothers Valhalla Memorial Park in North Hollywood (Burbank). In 2002 his recording of "When You Wish Upon a Star," used for many years as a Disney theme and heard over the closing credits of Spielberg's *Close Encounters of the Third Kind* (1977), was inducted into the Grammy Hall of Fame.

Standing next to him is John "Jimmie" Thach (1905–1981), later Admiral Thach, one of the great American aviators and tacticians who helped solve, amongst other things, the issue of Japanese Zero carrier fighter superiority with a flight formation known as the "Thatch Weave." Trained at Annapolis, he began his career as a communications officer in battleships but demonstrated early ability as a flyer, graduating from Pensacola at the top of his class. He joined Fighting Squadron 1 (VF-1B), based on North Island, and they were soon flying the new Curtiss F8C-4 "Helldivers." These fabric-covered biplanes had a maximum speed of 158 miles per hour, could operate up to 21,000 feet, carried a maximum 500-pound bomb load and were armed with two fixed .30 caliber forward firing guns and one rear-firing .50 caliber.

With the full blessing of the Navy, the pilots from the VF-1B squadron were involved with making *Hell Divers*, although they didn't receive any extra pay. Jimmie recorded a lot of flight hours for the film shoot, including one remarkable scene that required a ground loop after landing on a sandy beach (he nailed it in one take) and another for which he was asked to slow roll and then barely miss a hangar with an 80-pound camera on one wing. Once he began the roll, he discovered that the weight of the camera prevented him coming out of it and so he had to complete the fly-by upside-down. Not surprisingly, on climbing out of the cockpit he informed the director that particular take would have to do.

Thach would later fly combat missions during the Battle of Midway, become a flight instructor and operations officer, then command the *Sicily* during the Korean War and the *Franklin D. Roosevelt*. He was appointed rear admiral in 1955 with the *Valley Forge* as his flagship. Recognized for his contributions to antisubmarine warfare, he eventually became commander in chief of U.S. Naval Forces in Europe, and a full admiral in 1965. The frigate *Thach* was named in his honor.

Wallace Beery was no novice to a joystick, having already logged many hours in his three aircraft. Due to this movie, Beery would develop a personal fascination with naval aviation resulting in him receiving his own Navy wings and commission in 1934, based out of the Naval Reserve Aviation Base at Long Beach, California. An Academy Award winner in 1931 for *The Champ*, Beery had a film career that went back to 1913 with the Chicago film company Essanay. His last picture was *Big Jack* (1949), just before he died. Along the way he was married to Gloria Swanson and Rita Gilman. He probably lived longer than many people expected; not only did he have a legendary reputation for his drinking, but in 1929 he suffered a stroke while flight instructor to fellow actor and student pilot Al Roscoe in a six-seat cabin aircraft. Roscoe must have earned graduation on the spot, somehow coaching the spinning plane to a successful solo landing.

Herbert "Ducky" Duckworth was also at Midway on the *Lexington*, became the commanding officer of the Naval Air Station, Jacksonville, Florida, in 1947, and by 1951 was Rear Admiral, Director of Aviation Plans in the Office of the Chief of Naval Operations during the Korean War. Lt. Southwick also saw duty during World War II. He was Vice Admiral Calhoun's flag secretary at Pearl Harbor on the morning of December 7, 1941, and eventually became a rear admiral before his retirement in the 1950s.

(I am indebted for much of the material about Thach to Steve Ewing's fascinating biography *Thach Weave: The Life of Jimmie Thach,* Naval Institute Press: Maryland, 2004.)

32   J. W. Sandison was a commercial photographer in Bellingham, Washington, from 1904 to 1962. During his long career he maintained a portrait studio downtown on West Holly Street, as well as doing a considerable amount of work for business and industrial clients, local schools and newspapers. In January 1935, he evidently couldn't resist the call of the wild to the snowy slopes of Mount Baker to catch some rare animals far away from their usual habitat: movie stars.

There's a lot of snow in *Call of the Wild* and most of it was on Washington's Mount Baker that winter. On January 15, Clark boarded a Southern Pacific train in Los Angeles bound for that familiar city of Portland, Oregon, where he was roused out of bed at eight the next

32 Photographed by J.W. Sandison on Washington's Mount Baker, Clark and Jack Oakie look every fur-clad inch of their roles in *Call of the Wild* in January 1935 (courtesy Whatcom Museum Archive).

morning by a trio of journalists knocking on his compartment door. Clark was happy to sit with them and reminisce about his days in that town working at a department store and studying the craft of acting. He cheerfully reminded them that a dog, not Gable, was actually the star of this movie. Then the train whisked him on to Seattle, from where he was taken by car to the Leopold Hotel in Bellingham and from there to Glacier where he finally met up with director "Wild Bill" Wellman and some 60 cast and crew. Co-star Loretta Young had thought it prudent to order some winter pajamas from Wahl's Department Store before leaving Bellingham and chose a dainty, warm green corduroy pair.

Mount Baker is a 10,778-foot volcano that has been active six times between 1843 and 1880. In 1897 Jack Post had discovered the Lone Jack ledge up there (east of Glacier) that became the richest gold lode in the district, assaying out at nearly $11,000 per ton, and the railroad in to Glacier reached there in 1909 because of the subsequent logging boom. Skiing and hiking tourism had increased during the 1920s and a road, now State Route 542, was constructed up to a high shoulder known as Heather Meadows where a lavish lodge with 100 bedrooms had been built. The main building burned down in 1931 but enough buildings survived to provide accommodation for cast and crew and background for the exteriors of *Call of the Wild*.

Jack Oakie, the other snowbound actor in this photo, was close to Clark's age and had likewise started on the stage and then stepped onto the ladder of movie stardom in 1927 at the end of the silent era. Unlike Clark who remained with one studio (MGM) for most of his career, Oakie left Paramount when his contract ended in 1934 to freelance. It was a very successful move for him, and he appeared in over 85 films into the 1940s. Unrestrained by contract conditions, he was also able to branch into radio where he had his own show between 1936 and 1938. A very popular comic actor and a good friend of Clark's, he moved into television in the late fifties and sixties. Apart from his acting, Oakie became renowned for his sprawling ranch "Oakridge" in Northridge in the San Fernando Valley (formerly Barbara Stanwyck's 11-acre "Marwyck" ranch where she raised thoroughbreds jointly with Zeppo Marx). Oakie raised horses, too, but he also planted a citrus orchard and bred Afghan hounds. His Sunday afternoon pool parties at the English Manor–style house designed by Paul Williams attracted neighbors such as Lucille Ball and Desi Arnaz, Lionel Barrymore and William Holden and became legendary.

Whether or not Clark or his large St. Bernard co-star, Buck, were the real stars of this movie, both were completely upstaged in the end by the weather. Blizzard after blizzard snowed them in, cutting them off for days at a time until plows could clear the road. It was so cold that the oil in the cameras froze. Tempers ran short in equal ratio to the food. Then Clark started to become uncharacteristically careless with his punctuality and script preparation on set. He was turning up at eleven in the morning when the call had been for nine. Everyone, including Wellman, would be standing around waiting while slowly going blue with the cold. It didn't take long, given that conditions were already enough to try a saint, for Wellman's temper to snap. One day he just stood up nose to nose with Clark and threatened to alter his face, despite a difference of 50 pounds between them. After that it was Mr. Wellman and Mr. Gable, but the shoot got back on schedule.

33   Clark's mind wasn't on the job because it was on someone else: Loretta Young, one of four sisters who started out as extras in silent movies. Her older sister Elizabeth went on to have an acting career as Sally Blane. Loretta became a protégé of Colleen Moore at 14 and by the early 1930s she was earning $1000 a week and living with her family in a large colonial mansion in Bel-Air that her mother had designed.

Then she preceded Katharine Hepburn by falling madly in love with married Spencer Tracy, but as both were devout Roman Catholics it was all doomed to failure. Tracy had not long gone back to his wife, in fact, when a hurt and vulnerable Loretta became marooned up there in the snow with an equally vulnerable Clark, whose second marriage was already in trouble. Cut off from the outside world on the side of a mountain, acting out being in love with each other on camera with little chance of escaping from each other when the camera stopped rolling, they were what Clark himself would have described as sitting ducks. Just to see her fragile beauty in the photograph on the next page alongside Clark's rugged good looks is to sense the inevitability of it all.

By the time they came down from the mountain barely a week before the Academy Awards, an avalanche of rumor about their relationship had snowballed into town ahead of them and for once it was true. It wasn't long afterwards when Loretta and her mother were meeting Clark to break the news that she was pregnant. Unfortunately, not only was this a personal issue for the couple but two star careers were at stake due to the morals clauses then written into contracts. As both of them were about to leave for different film locations, a blanket of absolute secrecy quickly descended over the entire situation. It was so successful that the baby would grow to be a mother herself before it even began to be lifted.

33 Still on Mount Baker, Clark, Loretta Young and Reginald Owen enjoy a little recreational skiing (courtesy Whatcom Museum Archive).

Within days, Clark and his wife Ria separated and he moved into the Beverly Wilshire Hotel. Clark and Loretta stayed in telephone contact using code words but despite his repeated requests to see her, Loretta, afraid to go out in public, refused. Clark left for South America and a blonde, blue-eyed daughter was born in November while he was away. He visited whenever he could, but in mid–1936 Loretta placed the baby in an orphanage until re-adopting it a few months later as her own child, one with which she could be safely seen in public. Though quite a few people in Hollywood were never in doubt as to the father of the girl with the dimpled grin and the big ears, Judy grew up never knowing for sure. Even when she met and talked with Clark as a teenager, no one said a word. It wouldn't be until just before her marriage in 1958 that her husband-to-be confirmed her history, but she would wait until 1966 before Loretta finally admitted to her privately that Clark was indeed her father. The world had to wait for that news until after Loretta died in August 2000.

However, there are three people in this photograph so let us not forget the gentleman on the right, Reginald Owen, who was one of the great character actors of his time. Born in England in 1887, he began his career in silent movies in 1911 while remaining on the stage. It was Broadway that brought him to the U.S. in the early twenties before he moved to Hollywood. He appeared in over 120 films, including as Ebenezer Scrooge in the 1938 version of *A Christmas Carol*. He was one of only three actors who played both Sherlock Holmes and

Watson on film. Members of later audiences might recognize him as Admiral Boom in *Mary Poppins* and as General Teagler in *Bedknobs and Broomsticks*.

34 Clark had waxed lyrical in an interview in Portland on his way to Mount Baker about how much he was looking forward to working in MGM's *Mutiny on the Bounty*; although in later years he would consistently call it and *It Happened One Night* his two favorite films, the role of Fletcher Christian was another part he was initially unwilling to accept. For one thing, as you can see in this photograph, he had to wear knee britches; for another, he had to shave off that carefully cultivated moustache the ladies loved and wear his hair in a short pigtail. It was all a little too effeminate for Gable, whose rough masculine image was his trademark. To make matters worse, he'd be a lone American voice in a sea of British accents. Perhaps justifiably, he protested that the public would never believe him in the role of a first mate in the British Navy, and so for some time Clark's reply to MGM executive Irving Thalberg was a flat "No!"

It was the head of MGM's story department, Kate Corbaley, who finally persuaded Clark that the role would actually emphasize masculinity and independence, and he reluctantly agreed to venture onto the high seas, or at least the waters of the Pacific around the island of Catalina. Probably much to his own surprise, he ended up having the time of his life and so did audiences while watching the film.

For some 88 days, director Frank Lloyd cajoled, instructed and occasionally threatened cast and crew while they sailed around Catalina Island in a replica *Bounty* and then around a studio tank for the small-boat scenes with Bligh (Charles Laughton) and his marooned sailors. The cast was as fraught with friction as their historic counterparts. Laughton seemed unsettled by Clark and consequently developed a habit of not looking him in the eye when he delivered lines. Clark was a man of method and order within which lay his security and Laughton's technique put him right off his rhythm, frequently causing him to storm off the set in frustration. Laughton would then retire hurt to his bungalow and shooting would grind to a halt. Thalberg would fly in by seaplane to yell at Lloyd, who would yell back.

The problem was that with a female co-star Clark could rely on his charm and perhaps just a little on his reputation to establish rapport, while with a male co-star he preferred to establish a genuine off-screen friendship that would enable them to work smoothly and respectfully together on the set without undue rivalry. For Clark that meant hunting, shooting, fishing and real men who looked you right in the eye. Clearly, friendship with the moody, self-obsessed and sexually ambiguous Laughton was going to be out of the question so Clark socialized with the crew instead, reveling in the great outdoors he loved while improving his sailing skills, learning to climb rigging on very

34 In costume as Fletcher Christian, Clark is photographed on Catalina Island by a fan as he signs an autograph with that unmistakable Gable grin while shooting *Mutiny on the Bounty* (1935) (courtesy the Gable Archive).

35 Al Miller, a *Bounty* volunteer, standing alongside the original unrestored helm by which Clark stood on board the 1935 *Bounty* (courtesy HMS Bounty Organization LLC).

tall masts, fishing for sharks and partying in Avalon on the weekends. In the end, all that seething tension actually helped make the movie the outstanding character study it is. After all, Captain Bligh and Fletcher Christian were not friends; they were men from completely different areas of the rank and class spectrum of their time in violent opposition over management of the ship.

For a final 10 days, Laughton and a small group of actors were tossed around on a small boat in a studio tank, pulled to and fro by wires while being toasted by huge arc lights that imitated the tropical sun so effectively that the actor's makeup ran and their skin burned. Then Lloyd discovered that Eddie Quillan was acting the part of a crew member who historically had remained behind on the *Bounty* with Christian, and so they had to start all over again without him. "We have conquered the sea," cries Bligh at the end of their 3500-mile small-boat voyage to Timor with only a compass and sextant to guide them, and cast and crew were said to have wept at the words. It's not hard to understand why.

35–36 Although the ship that was converted to be the *Bounty* for the 1935 film no longer exists, its wheel (or helm) is still sailing the high seas. The real *Bounty* that was commissioned by the British Admiralty in 1787 to sail halfway around the world to Tahiti in search of breadfruit trees was a conversion of the coal transport *Bethia*. Likewise, the ship used to portray the *Bounty* in the 1935 movie was a conversion of a 117-foot-long, 142-ton two-masted schooner

36   The 1935 *Bounty* under sail (courtesy Catalina Island Museum).

named *Lily*, built of Douglas fir at San Francisco in 1882 by the Dickie Brothers for the West Coast lumber trade.

Realizing that their property department would be in need of some realistic sailing ships for large-scale movies such as *Mutiny on the Bounty*, and that they could now be had cheaply as they were replaced by steam power, MGM bought the *Lily* in 1934 for $10,000 with an eye to conversion. They already owned the three-masted fur-trading schooner *Ottilie Fjord* that had been the *Nanuk* for the film *Eskimo* and the *Hispaniola* in *Treasure Island*. For this film, the *Lily* would become the frigate *Pandora*.

Conversion work on the *Lily* was carried out at shipyards in Wilmington, California, using plans of the original *Bounty*. Because the *Lily*'s hull was far too narrow, new ribs were placed around the hull and covered with planking and then the gap between the hulls was filled with concrete as ballast. In place of her previous fore-and-aft rig, *Lily* was given three new masts and a square rig, along with four four-pound "cannons" along the aft section of the upper deck, two swivel guns forward and six aft. The work cost $50,000 and was carried out in 28 days, compared to the year it took to build the original *Bounty*. For the shipwreck scenes, they were hardly going to destroy such valuable work and so an exact, seaworthy 27-foot model of the ship powered by an automobile engine was built at the same time.

After *Mutiny on the Bounty*, the two ships were moored at Long Beach until the beginning of World War II, when they disappeared without trace. By then, however, the *Bounty*'s wheel had been removed by MGM for use as a prop on various sound stages. It eventually found its way in 1960 onto a new *Bounty* constructed by MGM for a remake starring Marlon Brando.

(For the details about the conversion of the *Lily* to the *Bounty*, I am indebted to Mark Winthrop's excellent site, http://www.winthrop.dk/bounty.)

37 The current *Bounty* was completely built as a new ship by the shipwrights Smith and Ruhland in Lunenberg, Nova Scotia, just the way she would have been built 200 years before and, like the 1935 ship, also according to the original *Bounty*'s drawings on file in the British Admiralty archives. When she was finished, Luis Marden hammered into the ship's hull a nail that he had brought up from the site where the original *Bounty* was sunk in the waters off Pitcairn Island. In August 1960, she was launched at Lunenburg before a crowd of over 20,000 people but nearly had a very short life. MGM wanted to literally burn the ship towards the end of filming just as the mutineers had done with the original *Bounty*, and it was only due to Marlon Brando's stubborn insistence otherwise that the ship survived the experience.

After filming was done, she was sailed on a world-wide promotional tour and then berthed at St. Petersburg, Florida, as a permanent tourist attraction. There she remained until 1986 when Ted Turner acquired her along with the MGM film library. In 1989, it was the *Bounty*'s turn to become the *Hispaniola* for Charlton Heston's remake of *Treasure Island* and the pirate ship in *Yellowbeard*.

In 1993, Turner donated the ship to the Fall River Chamber Foundation from whom it was purchased in 2001 by Robert Hansen and his HMS Bounty Organization LLC, the current owners, who had a dream to restore the vessel so that it would once again sail the oceans. By that time, the *Bounty* was in dire need of restoration and so she was slipped in Maine for the bottom to be replaced along with frames, running gear, engines, props and water tanks. Four years later, for *Pirates of the Caribbean II: Dead Man's Chest*, she had her rigging completely refitted and her sails replaced by Disney, in the same shipyards in Alabama where the *Black Pearl* was built, to appear as an 18th-century British warship.

After filming was completed, it was decided to take her back to Boothbay Harbor Shipyard in Maine to replace ribs and planking above the waterline, along with the stem, and to carry out an internal refit of the "tween" deck area to allow more cabin space for training crews and a new galley. Now com-

37 Standing watch at the restored 1935 wheel aboard the present HMS *Bounty* is Jesse Ludke (courtesy HMS Bounty Organization LLC).

38   The prints of Clark's hands and feet as they appear today in the forecourt of Grauman's Chinese Theatre on Hollywood Boulevard, where they were imprinted by Clark on January 20, 1937, with the help of Sid Grauman, director W.S. "Woody" Van Dyke and Jean Klossner (courtesy the Gable Archive).

pletely restored, she sailed in 2007 back to Lunenburg, Nova Scotia, and then on to England before returning along Bligh's original navigational path to Tahiti in 2008 for the 220th anniversary of *Bounty*'s first arrival there, before sailing on to Pitcairn Island and then returning to the U.S. In 2011 she is sailing to the U.K., Poland, Germany, Sweden and Norway.

Even though the *Bounty* has been carefully and lovingly cared for, the true thanks for her sailing again in open waters really belongs to those original shipwrights from Nova Scotia. "No one is building ships like this any more," Robert Hansen muses. "To construct this today would probably cost $10 million, maybe more. And that's if you could find a yard that would do it at all."

(I am indebted for much of this information to Margaret Ramsey, former executive director of the HMS Bounty Organization LLC, and to www.tallshipbounty.org.)

38   No trip to Hollywood is complete without visiting the forecourt of Grauman's Chinese Theatre to see the prints in cement of movie stars' hands and feet. Designed by Raymond Kennedy of the firm Meyer and Holler and opened in 1927 after 18 months work at a cost of $2,000,000, this theatre was the master-work of entrepreneur Sid Grauman, who had already built the Million Dollar Theatre and the Egyptian Theatre a few blocks down the street. Decorated with temple bells, pagodas and stone Heaven Dogs imported from China, the theater rises some 90 feet high with an entrance guarded by a 30-foot-high dragon carved from stone.

Grauman always claimed that the idea of placing prints of the stars in the forecourt paving occurred to him after he had accidentally walked into wet cement on the site. Mary

Pickford, on the other hand, claimed the idea came to her after seeing her dog Zorro run across a freshly poured driveway. However, Meyer-Holler's construction foreman Jean Klossner had a much longer tradition to fall back on in laying his own claim to originating the concept: three generations of his family had signed their work on Notre Dame Cathedral by pressing their hands into wet cement. Klossner had brought the tradition with him to America where his handprint had already signed off his work on a number of buildings around town including the Egyptian Theatre, the All-American Theatre, the Hollywood Masonic Lodge, and the Chinese Theatre where his signature and print can still be seen today.

Later known as "Mr. Footprint," Klossner was retained by Grauman after the theatre was opened to put into use his secret formula for a cement that remained pliable for 20 hours, enabling accurate prints to be pressed into it and mistakes to be corrected, yet would then set extremely hard without cracking and so preserve the detail of those imprints with a minimum of wear for decades. He personally supervised casting ceremonies until 1957, up until which no two print slabs had ever been made the same shape, size and color. So closely did he guard his formula, in fact, that when he died in 1965 he took the secret with him.

The first print-casting ceremony was for Mary Pickford and Douglas Fairbanks on April 30, 1927, hardly a surprise as Pickford and Fairbanks were the other two financial partners in the theatre venture along with Howard Schenck. Ten years later, Clark accepted an invitation to join a rapidly growing group of stars. A ceremony, the 33rd, was held on January 20, 1937, for both him and "Woody" Van Dyke. In the spirit of Clark's intense popularity, the largest crowd that had ever gathered at one of these ceremonies was there to watch him arrive from shooting *Parnell* at MGM to place his handprints and footprints into the wet cement slab. Then the prints had to be guarded for weeks after people were spotted hanging around the Chinese Theatre carrying hammers and chisels. The Gable crowd record remained, incidentally, until Doris Day's ceremony on January 19, 1961.

There are now approximately 195 sets of imprints in the forecourt of the Chinese Theatre, including not only prints of hands and feet but also of Harold Lloyd's glasses, Groucho Marx's cigar, John Wayne's fist, William S. Hart's guns, and the hoofprints of Roy Rogers' horse Trigger.

39–40 Few aircraft survive today that appeared in classic movies of the thirties, but there is a little yellow airplane at the New England Air Museum in Windsor Locks, Connecticut, that will remain forever associated with Clark Gable: the race plane that he "flies" in the movie *Test Pilot*. While Clark never actually flew this plane, of course, one can't help but feel that he would if he'd had the chance to learn. He certainly looks the part of Jim Lane, test pilot for the Drake

39 The restored *Silver Bullet*, the Marcoux-Bromberg plane that appears in the film *Test Pilot* as the No. 7 *Grant Special*, currently housed in the New England Air Museum (courtesy New England Air Museum).

Airplane Company, who loves life on the edge supported by his trusty mechanic Gunner, played by Spencer Tracy. Understandably, the machinery-loving Clark was in his element on *Test Pilot* and had a great time surrounded by high-powered engines and the men who worked on them and flew them. It was while making this film that he met Al Menasco, an engineer and former World War I test pilot who helped assemble the collection of planes for the film and who became one of Clark's lifelong friends. The film itself, with its actual footage of aerial pylon racing by well-known pilots of the time, is quite a piece of aerial archival history. Miraculously some of those planes survived and the *Marcoux-Bromberg Special* is one of them.

In all but the close-ups, the *Marcoux-Bromberg* is actually piloted by Earl Ortman on whom Clark's character in the movie is loosely based. Ortman was a well-known test pilot for civilian and military aircraft from the mid–1930s to the late 1940s, as well as being a record-holding race pilot. As Lane and Gunner do in the film, Ortman once carried out diving tests from 10,000 feet to 1,000 to prove the structural strength of an HM-1 experimental plane

for the military, increasing the speed of each dive until the wings actually ripped off, whereupon he calmly bailed out. Not surprisingly, much like Clark's pilot character, he was said to drink and smoke heavily and was inclined to be somewhat edgy.

The development of the *Marcoux-Bromberg Special* began in 1933 for the MacRobertson Air Race from England to Melbourne, Australia. Suggested by Melbourne Lord Mayor Harold Smith, and sponsored by wealthy confectionary manufacturer Sir Macpherson Robertson, the MacRobertson Trophy Air Race was announced well in advance as part of the Melbourne Centenary festivities. Supervised by the Royal Aero Club of England, the competing pilots would depart from the RAF Mildenhall base in East Anglia on October 20, 1934, and finish at Flemington Racecourse, Melbourne.

40   Clark posing as the heroic aviator on the hood of a Ford V-8 while in costume for *Test Pilot* (1938) (courtesy the Gable Archive).

Aircraft designers and builders all over the world were galvanized into action, as there was to be no limit on the type or size of participating aircraft. One of them was Keith Rider, an experienced Californian aircraft designer and builder, who began work in 1933 on an aircraft specifically designed for the race in a Los Angeles factory building that had been used for manufacturing coffins — rather a prediction of things to come. By August 1934, after many difficult months of work, the plane was ready for testing. An aluminum-skinned, 21' 8"–long, cantilever low-winged monoplane with retractable landing gear, it had spars of black walnut and its 25-foot wingspan was covered in mahogany plywood. Its supercharged Pratt & Whitney Wasp Jr. engine developed a massive 500 hp driving a two-bladed Hamilton Standard propeller. Rider estimated that the aircraft could complete the route in 44 hours but the plane crashed on its maiden takeoff, killing the pilot and damaging it sufficiently to end any hope of flying in the MacRobertson race.

When the plane was eventually repaired, two Douglas Aircraft engineers, Jack Bromberg and Harold Marcoux, persuaded Rider to hire the experienced Earl Ortman as his new pilot. On July 3, 1935, Ortman fulfilled their expectations by setting an inter-city record in the *Silver Bullet*, as the plane was now known because of its polished aluminum skin, flying from Vancouver to Agua Caliente in Mexico in 5 hours and 27 minutes. Now they were ready to race.

Racing airplanes against each other, either around circuits between pylons or across land or sea distances, developed into significant events during the first three decades of the 20th century, providing venues for testing and displaying rapid developments in aircraft design and speed. The first recognized air race was the 1910 Gordon Bennet International Air Race held in Belmont Park, New York, and the race that had the most impact on aircraft design for speed was the international Schneider Trophy for seaplanes first held in 1913. During the 1930s, there were two great annual races over land. The Bendix Trophy (begun in 1931) was a transcontinental race from Burbank, California, to Cleveland, Ohio, while the Thompson Trophy (begun in 1929) was a closed-course race; that is, planes flew laps ten miles long around pylons fifty feet high. A group usually consisting of eight planes took off only ten seconds apart and flew twenty laps in close proximity at speeds that by 1936 were over 220 miles an hour. Needless to say, Death was a frequent spectator.

In July 1936, Hal Marcoux purchased the *Bullet*, redesigning and rebuilding it in partnership with Bromberg and Ortman as a national air racer. By the time they were done, it was no longer really a Rider design and so was known from then as the *Marcoux-Bromberg Special*. Because of sponsorship by the Gilmore Oil Company, the plane was repainted cream with red trim.

That year, the National Air Races were transplanted from Cleveland to Los Angeles. After test flights of up to 312 mph and a forced pull-out dive where he reached 13.8 gs, Orton believed the plane was in the best flying condition he'd yet seen. In the qualifying trials for the Thompson Race, Ortman had the plane around the course at an average speed of 259 mph. He came in second. The team went back to the drawing board, reworked the fuselage, moved the cockpit a little further aft and fitted a much more powerful Pratt & Whitney engine with a three-bladed prop. Despite at one point flying too high and passing out from lack of oxygen, Ortman placed second in the Bendix. Then on September 6, he came in second in the Thompson Trophy Race, only two-tenths of a second behind the winner. The ensuing media publicity drew him to the attention of MGM who contracted him for *Test Pilot*.

The race scenes for the movie were shot over the actual pylon racing course at Cleveland Airport with which Ortman would have been quite familiar. They included other well-known Thompson Trophy pilots such as Paul Mantz and Frank Tomick. The *Marcoux Bromberg* was fitted with a smoke generator under the fuselage to imitate engine trouble. The later military test pilot scenes were shot at Langley and March Fields using the new Boeing YB-17.

As it turned out, this was the *Special*'s moment in the sun. Despite repeated Thompson Trophy attempts in 1938 and 1939, it would never again be so close to winning. The fastest recorded speed it flew around the Cleveland course was 307 mph in 1939, but by then the rumblings of war were spelling the end of circuit aircraft racing. When the *Special* was rolled into a hangar at Cleveland Airport for storage, its current engine had less than 40 hours flying time on it. After the war was over, two brothers from Cleveland bought the plane intending to race it again but the plans were shelved. In the mid–1950s, Rudy Profant discovered it packed in pieces in a trailer and bought them intending to restore it but that never happened, either. Fortunately, in 1978 the New England Air Museum finally took over ownership and began an immediate restoration program which was finally completed in October 1984, when the *Marcoux-Bromberg Special* joined the Museum display in some excellent company. Next to it sits the *Laird Solution*, winner of the first Thompson Trophy in 1930, and on the other side is the North American P51-D that captured the Thompson Trophy in 1948. The *Marcoux-Bromberg Special* is a miraculous survivor of a unique group of aircraft and of an era in aviation history that provided an important impetus to the development of aircraft design and technology. Clark would be proud to be back sitting in the cockpit.

41 Twelve years later would find Clark sitting in a very different cockpit: that of the *Mike Brannan Special* on the Indianapolis Raceway during the running of the Indianapolis 500. The historic Raceway was one of the exterior and race scene locations for *To Please a Lady*, his eighth film with director Clarence Brown. Clark plays Mike Brannan, a ruthless midget racing car driver who is involved in a crash with another car whose driver is killed. Stanwyck plays journalist Regina Forbes who successfully crusades to have Mike banned from racing. Blacklisted, Mike finds work in Joie Chitwood's stunt driving show. By the time he can finance another full-sized race car, he and Regina are involved in a complicated romance that will need to survive the forthcoming Indy 500 race.

Short-track midget car racing was highly popular from the mid-thirties through to the mid-sixties in America. Many Indianapolis 500 drivers earned their wheels training on dirt tracks in midgets, graduating to the more powerful

41 In May 1950, to publicize the film *To Please a Lady*, Clark is presented with a trophy by Barbara Stanwyck who once said that no matter what Clark's age, he'd never grow old. Clark is sitting in the cockpit mock-up of the *Mike Brannan Special* used for race close-ups (courtesy the Gable Archive).

sprint cars before moving up to the full-size championship cars. So, the shooting of racing scenes for this movie was spread over the Carroll Speedway in LA, the one-mile dirt fairground track at Del Mar, California, and the Arlington Race Track at Arlington in Texas. Then the finale was shot during the running of the actual Indianapolis 500 in May of 1950.

The *Mike Brannan Special* that Clark is seen driving was actually the *Don Lee Special*, a Kurtis-Kraft 2000 Offy that had been built in 1948 as #319 by Frank Kurtis at his shop in Glendale, California. This car had been built for LA businessman Tommy Lee, who had inherited his father Don's Cadillac dealership, some radio and TV stations, and the Don Lee Coach and Body works that built custom autos for Hollywood stars, and it was actually the third of thirteen KK2000s the Kurtis shop would build. During the previous season, MGM had closely followed and filmed Rex Mays racing in his #17 Wolfe Special, another KK2000, as the Brannan car for the movie but then Mays was killed and the car damaged in a tragic accident in November 1949. So the studio located and bought the Lee car, a lookalike Kurtis, as a substitute.

Having shot their midget footage in California, MGM needed footage of a longer race. They found Elbert "Babe" Stapp's Arlington Downs track at Arlington, Texas, and persuaded Stapp to hold an MGM Sweepstakes on April 30 for them to film. After all, the presence of stars like Gable and Stanwyck would turn the event into a sell-out. They shipped down the KK2000, and after a little redecoration it became the #17 *Mike Brannan Special*. Driver and mechanic "Bud" Rose, whose real name was Harry Eisele and who closely resembled Clark, was his stand-in during several days of filming. Another well-known race driver, Johnny Parsons, laid out the car movements on the track for the scenes. However, constant rain and bad weather along with a car crash and the consequent repairs to vehicles slowed up the shooting. The actual race was finally run as planned, though on a wet track before a small crowd, and then everyone packed up on May 3 and moved to the Indianapolis Speedway.

The Indianapolis scenes feature an on-track battle between Brannan's car and that of three-time Indy winner Mauri Rose, playing himself. Rose earned a memorable place in the picture when there was a fire during a pit stop. He was able to rejoin the race, though, leaving his chief mechanic to frantically struggle out of his burning pants so he could save the $2000 in his pockets. MGM reverted to their original plan of using the now-rebuilt *Wolfe Special* as the Brannan vehicle, driven in the actual 500 race by Joie Chitwood. "Bud" Rose staged some initial scenes as the Gable lookalike in the Don Lee car, but he failed to qualify and joined Gable in watching from the sidelines to cheer on Johnny Parsons who went on to win the 1950 event despite the bad weather that had followed them north, causing the race to be called on the 138th lap. The *Wolfe Special* was placed fifth.

The *Mike Brannan/Don Lee Special* was eventually sold to Joe Gemsa in California where it won the 500-mile race at Riverside in 1958 as the *Clark Gable Special*, naturally driven by none other than "Bud" Rose. It was then sold to Vern Erwin and is now with Tom Malloy, restored to its 1948 #35 Don Lee colors. The *Wolfe Special* #77 had placed fifth at Indianapolis in 1949 (driven by Joie Chitwood) before Mays' accident, and it went on to race at Indianapolis again in 1952 when it was placed tenth. The car was still mobile in the early 1990s when it made appearances at occasional vintage meets.

(I am indebted for much of the information in this section to Lou Brooks, in his 2004 article "From Race Car to Movie Star: The Strange Story of the Don Lee Special," www.loubrooks.com.)

42 Joie Chitwood, who had just raced around the Indianapolis Speedway standing in for Clark, was not only known for his skills on the track but was perhaps even more famous as the owner of a widely popular daredevil stunt-driving show. Born in St. Joseph, Missouri, George Rice "Joie" Chitwood (1912–88) was orphaned at 14 and did odd jobs around Kansas until he learned to be a welder, then worked as a mechanic until he got his break driving a car at the Winfield Speedway in Kansas in 1934. It was the beginning of a long career behind the wheel.

Between 1940 and 1950, he competed in the Indy 500 seven times, finishing fifth in '46, '49 and '50. He is also said to have been the first man to wear a seat belt at the Indy, no doubt inspired by accidents such as that of Rex Mays who had been thrown out of his vehicle to his death. In 1943, out of work as a race driver because war-time gas and tire rationing had restricted the sport, Joie bought Lucky Teter's Hell Drivers stunt show after Lucky's car missed a 125-foot jump and his luck ran out. Never having done daredevil driving before, Joie had to figure it out for himself but by the time he retired from racing in 1950, he'd done so well that the Joie Chitwood Thrill Show was a resounding success. More than 110,000 people

42   Not looking anything like a race car driver, a cheerful Clark is presented with his official Joie Chitwood auto daredevil racing helmet by none other than Joie Chitwood himself in May 1950 (courtesy the Gable Archive).

packed Soldier Field in Chicago for one performance alone. In 1978, Joie set a world record by driving a Chevrolet Chevette for 5.6 miles on just two wheels. Eventually, there were five Chitwood show units touring America thrilling audiences with their driving stunts, and an estimated 25 to 30 million people saw the show during its 55-year run.

One of the show's advertising banner headlines ran with photos of the Chitwood stunt team, sometimes known as the Danger Angels, and the tag-line "These men are marked for DEATH!" Joie came close enough; he once needed 50 stitches in his neck after missing a ramp in Arlington, Texas. After *To Please a Lady*, Joie worked in a number of other films as either a stunt driver or driving coordinator, and in 1973 he was the stunt coordinator for the James Bond film *Live and Let Die*. He was also a car safety consultant, intentionally crashing cars to test their structure resistance. By 1965 he claimed to have crashed more than 3000 vehicles. He was inducted into the National Sprint Car Hall of Fame in 1993.

43   Clark was feted over that Memorial Day weekend during which every Indianapolis 500 race takes place. He appeared in the pre-race parade with Barbara Stanwyck, and drove the

43 Shaking hands with Clark at the 1950 Indianapolis 500 is driver Pat Flaherty sitting in 59, the *Granatelli Sabourin Special.* Standing around him are, from left to right, Andy Granatelli, unknown, Joe Granatelli, unknown (partially obscured), Fred Fallbush, unknown (dark glasses), and Vince Granatelli who is partly obscured behind Clark on the right (courtesy Indianapolis Motor Speedway Photo Operations).

Mercury pace car. He and his new wife, Lady Sylvia Ashley, were said to be the guests for the month of Anton Hulman, Jr., who had bought Indianapolis Motor Speedway for $750,000 in 1945. Clark immersed himself in the atmosphere and met as many of the drivers and owners as he could. Naturally enough, they wanted to meet him, too, and Pat Flaherty and the already famous Granatelli brothers were no exception.

Red-haired, slim, six-foot tall George Francis "Pat" Flaherty (1926–2002) had started out as a hot rod track racer in California, before becoming part of Andy Granatelli's Hurricane Hot Rod Association after he moved to Chicago in 1948. Granatelli introduced Pat to the Indy Speedway in 1949, although that time they didn't qualify. He had started in this 1950 race in a new Granatelli "Offy" that was the first Indy roadster to have independent front suspension. It was known as the *Granatelli Sabourin Special* because, while the vehicle had actually been built by the Granatellis, the money for the project had come from Dr. Raymond Sabourin, a prominent New York chiropractor and one of the founders of the Auto Racing Fraternity Foundation.

After further starts in 1953 and 1955, Flaherty finally won the Indy in 1956 dressed in slacks and T-shirt, protected only by his helmet decorated with a green shamrock, driving the first Roadster entirely designed and built by A.J. Watson, owned by John "Jack" Zink. After winning a number of other championships and racing again at Indianapolis in 1959, Flaherty retired from motor racing to become expert in another form of racing altogether — pigeons.

The Granatelli brothers surrounding the car here with Clark became the pioneers of the "speed shop" concept, eventually creating a multi-million dollar business based on marketing automotive parts. Along the way, they became a major force in American motorsports. Growing up in Depression-era Chicago, the brothers earned their keep from an early age, giving jump starts to stalled cars on winter mornings with the help of a battery they hauled around the streets. Soon they were all working multiple jobs, pooling their money until Joe was finally old enough to get a job as a mechanic. He taught Andy to service cars and they both taught Vince. They began racing cars on rural roads for the prize money, and before long they were winning enough to open Andy's Super Service just off Lake Shore Drive. Their business was a huge success until they were completely stripped in 1944 during a robbery.

With no insurance they started over from scratch, devoting the new business strictly to speed. Soon they were contracting out their sales services for other companies while developing a superior reputation for their engineering expertise building high-performance Ford V-8 engines. It was probably inevitable that they would quickly move beyond driving to promotion, founding the Hurricane Hot Rod Racing Association and putting tens of thousands of racing fans in the seats of Chicago's Soldier Field and many other tracks night after night.

Considering the rapid growth of their business and their reputation, it was probably inevitable that the Granatellis would one day show up at the Indianapolis 500 along with their chief mechanic, Earl Johnson. From 1946 to 1954, they entered cars under their Grancor (Granatelli Corporation) name; within a few years, the business was turning over some $14 million a year as they became masters of the concept of mass merchandising high-performance auto parts. It was enough to tempt them away from racing. Andy went to California in 1957 where with Joe he purchased the supercharger business of Paxton Products Corporation and came into contact with Clark again, fitting a supercharger to his Thunderbird.

For the next few years, the brothers pushed the high-performance benefits of their superchargers, setting more than 300 land speed and endurance records. Chrysler were impressed and brought them in to help redesign the famed Indianapolis Novis engine, and soon the brothers returned to the Brickyard to race it. Then South Bend, Indiana, car producer Studebaker offered Andy a CEO position; he took a product by the name of STP, short for Scientifically Treated Petroleum, and made it famous. Granatelli mass-marketed his product in ways no one had quite seen before, making the logo of white STP letters on a red oval about as famous as a Coca-Cola sign. He and his racing team even wore white suits completely covered with STP patches. The logo became so ubiquitous that when Neil Armstrong and his fellow astronauts went to the moon, the New York Times published a cartoon showing him stepping onto the surface to be greeted with an STP sign. Andy was also instrumental in the development of the Studebaker Avanti.

The Granatellis continued to race at Indianapolis for some 30 years, winning in 1969 with Mario Andretti driving and again in 1973 with Gordon Johncock. By 1970 they were also racing on the European Grand Prix circuit. They introduced the revolutionary STP-Turbocars in 1967 and 1968, brought the first modern four wheel drive to U.S. racing, designed a side-by-side (engine and driver) chassis for ideal weight distribution and developed an air brake flap for added safety. For many years, Joe, Andy, and Vince continued to be leaders by example. Joe passed away in 2003; Andy still resides in Southern California and Vincent is in Arizona.

44   When he sat down with Danny Kladis that weekend, little did Clark know he was talking to a driver who would one day hold a unique place in racing history. When Danny died in April 2009, at age 92, he was the oldest living Indy 500 starter.

Danny began driving midget cars in Chicago in the mid-thirties, pausing to become a pilot during World War II and then returning behind the small wheel to become Mississippi Valley Midget Racing Association champion in 1946, as well as holding a number of other titles. Actually, no one knows for sure exactly how many titles Danny did win during his life; he was said to have won 32 track championships in Iowa alone.

His first start in the Indy 500 was in 1946, having been hired by the Granatelli brothers. It was the first 500 experience for them all. Danny was driving a 1935 front-drive Ford V-8 Miller with a Mercury engine fitted with the brothers' own Grancor head. Starting from the back, Kladis was running in 16th place when he made a pit stop for fuel. No sooner did he return to the track, though, than the car lost power and stopped. Someone in the pit had forgotten to turn the fuel safety valve back on. Unwittingly the Granatellis towed the car off the track, thereby disqualifying themselves because they had left the course.

Although he returned to the Brickyard over the next 10 years, Kladis never qualified again, although he drove 50 laps in the 1954 Indy for Spider Webb as a relief driver. However, he was still racing on other tracks and winning in other events well into the 1960s, despite at various times breaking arms, collarbones and his back. In 1962 he was the United Auto Racing Association driving champion. Often seen at Raceway Park, just a short distance from his Chicago home, Kladis entertained crowds by taping silver dollars over his eyes and then driving blind around the track at close to racing speed. His son George was the 1971 UARA champion, and they would sometimes both do the silver dollar trick, driving simultaneously in opposite directions around the track. In 2007, he was inducted into the National Midget Auto Racing Hall of Fame.

Kladis also continued to maintain his pilot status, flying both commercial aircraft and chartered corporate jets. When he wasn't racing, he worked as a supervisor in the Chicago Ford plant that built Pratt & Whitney air engines where Howard Hughes had the eight engines constructed for his *Spruce Goose.* A great raconteur, Kladis used to say that the Hughes engineers and occasionally Hughes himself would call him when they had questions. He also used to say that Andy Granatelli called him the Wonder Boy of the Speedway

44   Race driver Danny Kladis chatting with Clark at the Indianapolis 500 in May 1950 (courtesy Indianapolis Motor Speedway Photo Operations).

because it was a wonder every time he came around again. In the long run, Danny Kladis did come around again to win his race; he outlived all the other competitors.

45 After Clark's divorce from Lady Sylvia was finalized, he evidently didn't want to sit around the ranch and mope. When his agency MCA negotiated a deal for him to appear in *Never Let Me Go* in England, he seized the chance to leave early (May 6, 1952) for France on board the *Liberte*. On the way over, he used his shipboard time to read the script for *Mogambo*, most of which would be shot in Africa under the direction of John Ford.

Eventually, Clark had to leave behind the romantic spring in Paris for the more uncomfortable London of June. He settled into the Dorchester Hotel and began work at the Boreham Wood studios on *Never Let Me Go* which was being directed by one good friend, Delmer Daves, and produced by another, Clarence Brown. His co-star was the beautiful Gene Tierney who had been invited by Brown to play the Russian ballerina who marries Gable's foreign correspondent character only for him to be deported and have to abandon her. Somewhat reprising the plot of his much earlier *Comrade X*, Clark then has to resort to sailing across the North Sea and impersonating a Russian officer in order to sneak back into the country and help her to escape.

Most of the boat scenes were shot off the coast of Cornwall in and around Mevagissey, while Mullion Cove Harbour on The Lizard stood in for the Russian harbor of Tallinin. The night beach scenes were shot at Lusty Glaze Beach ("a place to view blue boats" in old Cornish) in

Newquay. The days of Cornish smugglers might have been long gone, but Tierney discovered to her dismay that there were till some pirates left; they stole $8,000 worth of her jewelry while she was in Newquay. Maybe it was a sign. Clark and Tierney had to stay at the Polurrian Hotel, the first hotel built on The Lizard, while they waited for weather that repeatedly turned bad, causing the filming schedule to fall further behind. Clark became bored and took to flying to Paris on the weekends to see his girl of the week, Suzanne Dadolle d'Abadie, a model for Schiaparelli.

When shooting was over, Clark decided to turn the trip to Africa for *Mogambo* into a vacation, and after *Mogambo* costume fitting in London he left again for France on September 20.

45 In this July 1952 photograph taken by one of the crew members on board, Clark is seen lining up for lunch at sea off the coast of Cornwall during one of the few days it didn't rain while making *Never Let Me Go* (courtesy the Gable Archive).

46–47 There was a reason Carr Hartley was involved with *Mogambo*. Once a man with a serious reputation as a big game hunter, he was now renowned for his skill in capturing animals alive for zoos and for filmmaking purposes. A big man (240 pounds), multi-lingual, a crack shot and a skilled bushman with some 30 years' experience, Hartley had stood

46 Taking a break during the shooting of *Mogambo* are Clark and Ava Gardner with John Ford (on the left in baseball cap) and Carr Hartley (standing to the right in safari jacket and hat) (with permission from Roy Carr-Hartley).

up to bull elephants with an empty gun and punched a charging lioness in the jaw. Needless to say, he was a man without fear. By the time the *Mogambo* convoy arrived, his family was running a large cattle farm operation and supplying most of the major zoos in the world with animals, while he was a wild animal consultant and trainer for film crews. He also hunted down as many Mau Mau terrorists as he could. The *Mogambo* troupe arrived in Kenya on the heels of the vicious and bloody Mau Mau terrorist uprising that had taken place the previous year.

The making of *Mogambo*, a remake of Clark's earlier film *Red Dust*, had prompted the biggest African location film venture attempted to that time. For the sake of authenticity MGM

47 Clark demonstrating his affinity with animals at the Carr Hartley Ranch before shooting for *Mogambo* began. The baby rhinoceros and elephant would appear in the film (with permission from Roy Carr-Hartley).

put together the largest safari East Africa had ever seen, and it had seen a lot of them. Scheduled for a 67-day location shoot, the logistics were nothing short of mind-boggling. It took more than eight days for the column of 50 trucks to travel the thousand miles to the Kagera River through country where daytime temperatures could reach 130 degrees.

When they reached the river, the crew set up a camp of some 300 tents, including accommodation and dining quarters, wardrobe and makeup departments, recreation tent, a hospital complete with x-ray equipment, and even a lock-up just in case. They built an 1,800-yard airstrip in five days so that supplies and mail could be flown in and film stock flown out. The whole site was guarded by a 30-man police force that could call on nearby British military posts in case of trouble. MGM even persuaded friendly local witch-doctors to cast protection spells on the locale.

They should have cast protection spells on the cast and crew as well. John Ford and Clark had diametrically opposite points of view about how to shoot a movie. Clark liked to prepare from a script; Ford had a very fluid attitude about a script, to say the least. Clark was a star with experience who figured he knew if his scene hadn't gone well and needed doing over; Ford considered he had the right of veto and it wasn't up for discussion. Needless to say, there was more than one explosion and walk-out by both parties. Ava Gardner found she was pregnant and was flown out at one point for hospitalization, and John Ford had to be treated for eyesight problems and amoebic dysentery. A rhino took exception to a Jeep in which Ava, Clark and Grace Kelly were riding and punched holes in it, but they were luckier than three other crew members who were killed when their vehicle crashed on a track. Finally, Clark nearly fell backwards over a cliff and had to be hauled back up on the end of a rope.

Understandably, Ford's mood grew darker and he began re-writing scenes so they could be shot back on a soundstage in England. In late January 1953, they all packed up and returned there for the shooting of interiors and post-production through February. With nothing to distract them now, Ford and Clark's hostility broke into the open until Clark flatly refused to work with or speak to him again. Finally, with producer Sam Zimbalist acting as referee, an uneasy truce was maintained until work was completed in April at a final cost of just over $3,000,000. Clark ended up admiring Ford's work, but it was from a great distance.

48   Despite that typical smile, Clark had by now become extremely disillusioned with the way in which MGM was managing his post-war career. Yet, he put on one last parade for them and acted out his role of the MGM star for what would be the last time. With the working title of *Holland Deep*, this film of the World War II Dutch underground resistance movement was also shot on location and so, after a few weeks of vacation in Europe and story conferences and wardrobe fittings in London, Clark flew with KLM over to Amsterdam on September 23, 1953.

Taking as much advantage of Clark's presence as they could, MGM had decided to stage a week-long goodwill tour through Holland prior to the start of filming. So, after being greeted by huge crowds and an eager press contingent at Amsterdam, Clark traveled on to Delft and then to Rotterdam where at the zoo he was presented with lion cubs Mogambo and Gable. As he held them, one cub nipped him and the other urinated on him. Seeing the keeper returning with a Bengal tiger, Clark and his two publicity assistants rushed into the nearest bar to escape and clean up only to discover that the name of the place was the Lion d'Or (Golden Lion). "I've had enough lions for one day," Clark quipped as they left.

On arriving in Maastricht, near the border with Germany and Belgium, Clark was met by a crowd of 8000 cheering people and a parade of tanks and guns to celebrate the anniversary of World War II American troops liberating the town. Champagne toasts were offered and speeches were made, including one by Clark expressing his gratitude for the welcome and

48 Once more with animals, Clark is presented with two lion cubs (named Mogambo and Gable) while visiting Rotterdam's zoo on the way to working on *Betrayed* (courtesy the Gable Archive).

claiming kinship with them through his mother. It was a worthy piece of public relations spin considering his ancestry was German, but perhaps he was trying to deflect any questions about his name before they started. The crowd loved it and cheered madly, and a pretty girl was chosen to kiss him on behalf of all the women in the crowd. Then they moved on through Utrecht and The Hague and some other cities and towns, before returning to Amsterdam to begin work. The tour was a remarkable success.

Of course, the trip wasn't just about public relations; it also allowed the chance for some location scouting; Clark, his co-star Lana Turner, and the other members of the cast and crew would return to some of these places a few weeks later. While working in and around Arnhem, Clark and *Colliers* photographer Martin Harris came up with the idea of testing just how well Clark was remembered after all the excitement of only a few weeks ago, and so Clark dressed up as a local barge hand and wandered around the streets. He stopped by a few fruit stands, leaned on some lamp-posts and mingled with pedestrians. No one gave him a second look for an hour, but then a pair of incredulous young women on bicycles spotted him and asked for autographs. In early November, he was back in Maastricht shooting scenes at the Butter Market and inside the local second-century church. Staying in a castle 10 miles out of town, Clark denied rumors that he was going to marry Suzanne Dadolle d'Abadie and live in Europe.

As it turned out, Clark was homesick for his ranch and, after interiors were shot at the studios in England, he made sure he was home for Christmas. This was his last movie for MGM. Despite their enticements to sign another contract, Clark quietly drove out of the

49 In a rare cross-cultural meeting of film royalty, the king of Hollywood meets the empress of Chinese film, Li Lihua, at the Kowloon Ferry Terminal, while he is in Hong Kong to shoot exteriors for *Soldier of Fortune* (December 3, 1954) (courtesy David Wells).

50 Clark and Li Lihua in conversation on board a ferry with an unknown woman (courtesy David Wells).

studio gates for the last time on March 3, 1954, with no fanfare or official farewell.

49–52 Gable arrived in Hong Kong about November 17, 1954, after passing through Tokyo, for exterior shooting of *Soldier of Fortune*. In the film he plays Hank Lee, an American smuggler and soldier of fortune living in Hong Kong who helps an American woman rescue her photojournalist husband held captive in Communist China. Director Edward Dmytryk commented candidly that Ernest K. Gann's book was a "potboiler," but he thought it one of the better ones. Although it sounds like it should be an action movie, *Soldier of Fortune* is actually a widescreen romance set against the colorful CinemaScope backdrop of Hong Kong which really acts as a third co-star in itself.

Eighteen other people traveled with Clark in the 20th Century–Fox

51 Clark and Li Lihua at the wheel of the ferry (**courtesy David Wells**).

52 Clark and Li Lihua at a Hong Kong restaurant with an unknown man (courtesy David Wells).

group for a 28-day location shoot; among them were Michael Rennie, Alex D'Arcy and Gable's makeup man from MGM, Don Roberson. Clark's co-star Susan Hayward was not able to leave the U.S. at the last minute because her ex-husband took out an injunction against her leaving with the children, so another member of the party was Hayward's double, Dale Logue, who was used in long shots. (She continued as Hayward's double in the future films *Back Street* and *Where Love Has Gone*.)

Clark was said to have initiated the get-together with Li Lihua because she was the one and only actress he was interested in meeting in Hong Kong. Her parents had been famous Beijing opera performers and she had begun her training when she was 11 and made her first film at 15, becoming an instant star. Her movie career spanned three decades of diversified roles. Although she was predominantly known for her strong feminist characters, amongst which were a number of femme fatales, she also played the occasional comic role. Arriving in Hong Kong in 1949, she was soon interviewed for *Life*; she had her own production company by 1954. She starred in the first color movie made in Hong Kong, *Blood Will Tell* (1955); her only Hollywood starring role was in *China Doll* (1956) with Victor Mature. She returned to Hong Kong to work for the Shaw Brothers in 1960 and starred in a number of their blockbusters, such as *The Magnificent Concubine*. In 1964 and 1969 she won Best Actress at the Golden Horse Film Awards. Although she immigrated to the U.S. in 1972, she now lives again in Hong Kong.

While Clark was working in Hong Kong, he also had to cope with rumors (trumped up by eager journalists back in America) that he and Marilyn Monroe might marry. A photo had been released of them dancing together at a party, and he had supposedly sent her roses when she was hospitalized shortly after. Clark just laughed off the stories, knowing that in fact a very different woman was waiting for him. When he did eventually arrive back in Los Angeles in mid–December 1954, Kathleen Spreckels was there to meet him. However, he had to leave within a few days for Durango, Mexico, to work on *The Tall Men*. When he returned, he and Kathleen were married secretly on July 11, 1955, in Minden, Nevada.

53 Perhaps he thought it would be a good idea at the time because Raoul Walsh would be directing again, but Clark said "yes" when he should have said "no" to this poor man's *Gone with the Wind* co-starring Yvonne De Carlo.

While he was working, Clark and Kathleen stayed at the Belle-

53 Looking the epitome of southern gentility, Clark arrives with Kathleen for the shooting of a scene for *Band of Angels* near Baton Rouge, Louisiana, in January 1957 (courtesy the Gable Archive).

54 The ruins of the Cottage Plantation House near Baton Rouge, Louisiana, one of the locations for *Band of Angels* (with permission from Colleen Kane).

mont Hotel in Baton Rouge, Louisiana. Kathleen followed her usual pattern of shopping and socializing with the local people, including Governor Long and his wife, from whom there was no shortage of invitations. She also visited Natchez where she was presented with the keys to that city. On February 1, Kathleen threw a birthday party for Clark at the Baton Rouge Country Club to which all the cast members were invited to find that the dishes on the menu were named after them.

54 Based on a novel by Robert Penn Warren, much of *Band of Angels* was shot near Baton Rouge at the magnificent Cottage, a plantation (reputedly haunted) that was destroyed by fire three years after the film shoot, and at the Poplar Grove Plantation where a field of sugar cane was ignited for a fire scene.

Built in 1824 by Col. Abner Duncan as a wedding gift for his daughter Frances and son-in-law Frederick Conrad, the 22-room Cottage plantation house was once considered one of the finest in the area. However, a series of events led to the house's reputation of being haunted. At about 10 in the morning of Sunday, February 27, 1859, four boilers of the steamboat *Princess* exploded simultaneously just after it left Baton Rouge adjacent to the Cottage Plantation. Carrying 400 people, the *Princess* promptly caught fire and drifted onto the shore by the house. Nearly 200 people were killed or injured. Many of the survivors, some terribly burned, were pulled ashore by plantation slaves and tended on the front lawn by the Conrad family who laid out bedsheets covered in flour with which burns patients were dusted. Many of them died there, and it is said that white dust can still be seen rising into the air around the ruins.

Only a few years later, during the Civil War, the house was occupied and stripped by the Union Army, abandoned by the Conrads, and eventually converted to a yellow fever hospital. After the war and Conrad's death, the house was occupied by the family's tutor and secretary, Angus Holt, who took over as manager of the plantation. Holt became quite eccentric as the years went by. For many years after his death in 1880, his ghost was said to still maintain a watch over the property. Nevertheless, the Conrads restored the house during the 1920s and by the 1950s it was open to the public as a museum of the Civil War era and was used as a setting for a number of films, including *Band of Angels*. However, its reputation for hauntings and strange events remained and it came as little surprise to many that when the house was mysteriously struck by lighting and burned down on February 18, 1960, firefighters reportedly saw the ghost of Holt at one of the upper windows.

55 For about two weeks in January 1957, shooting took place along the levee at Sardine Point, near the neighboring town of Addis, where locals were employed as extras on board the sternwheeler *Gordon C. Greene* which was renamed *River Queen* for the occasion. People came from miles around to get hired, and competition for the roles was fierce. Joycelyn Gauthreaux was one of the lucky ones, although sometimes they wondered about that. The 6:30 A.M. start usually meant leaving home around 4 A.M. to arrive at the Heidelberg Hotel in time to get dressed in their costume before being taken by Greyhound bus to the location. Often they didn't return to the hotel until well after dark. It was usually bitterly cold, with temperatures hovering in the twenties, and windy. Sometimes it was too cold or cloudy for any shooting, so the extras sat around and played cards. Clark would go off to shoot quail.

Working on the set and meeting Clark Gable was an experience Gauthreaux would remember for the rest of her life. She and fellow extra Gloria Wilbert recalled that he was just a "regular guy" who would talk, sign autographs and didn't seem to mind having his photo

55 Mrs. Joycelyn Gauthreaux's pay slip showing her employment as an extra for *Band of Angels* at the sum of $10 a day, less tax (courtesy Addis Historical Society, Addis, LA).

taken. So, one cold morning while they were all waiting to start shooting, Gauthreaux approached Clark as he waited in his warm car and asked him if she could take his picture and, sure enough, he readily agreed as long as he didn't have to get out of the car.

Filming locally also meant that crowds of spectators turned up to try and glimpse the stars working, and complaining about it brought Clark and De Carlo together. She observed that the closest fans could get to the set was to the "honey wagons" parked on the outskirts, and so they had taken to waiting there in order to photograph whoever would go in and out. When she commented they were taking photos of her zipping up her fly, Clark laughed uproariously and they were friends from then on.

Despite all the popular attention while it was being made, *Band of Angels* didn't attract the same crowds to watch it on the screen. Clark never worked with Walsh again. However, although Gauthreaux's work ended up on the cutting room floor, this film was the start of another extra's career: Dot Bourgeois from Zachary (*née* Dorothy Smith from Pride). Five years later she would be better known as Donna Douglas, playing Elly Mae Clampett on TV's *The Beverly Hillbillies*.

56   After he graduated from Classen High School in Oklahoma City in 1932, Herschel Jordan decided to move to the much more exciting Los Angeles to live a little and earn some money before starting college. He found a job tending bar at the luxurious 1921 Myron Hunt–designed Ambassador Hotel. Home of the Cocoanut Grove nightclub and Academy Award ceremonies, later to be the site of Robert F. Kennedy's assassination in 1968, the Ambassador during the 1930s was the haunt of many a film star, including Clark.

At this time, Herschel had dark hair and a thin moustache and Clark frequently referred to him with a laugh as "my double," and that is how he signed this photograph for him. Two years later Herschel returned home where he eventually graduated from the University of Oklahoma with a degree in journalism and after World War II, in which he served as an Army Air Corps captain with an anti-submarine unit in the Cayman Islands, he worked for an Oklahoma City newspaper for almost 40 years. Herschel treasured his photo of Clark Gable until his death in 2008 at the age of 93.

56   Clark autographed and presented this photograph to Ambassador Hotel barman Herschel L. Jordan in 1936 (courtesy the Gable Archive).

Military Life

57   Immediately after the Japanese had attacked Pearl Harbor on December 7, 1941, Carole Lombard felt that she and Clark should do whatever they could to be of service to their country. She considered joining the Red Cross or one of the women's armed service branches and she wanted Clark to enlist. But at 41, a tad older than your average recruit, and earning $7,500 a week at the top of the movie actor ladder, he had hedged a little and instead joined the Hollywood Victory Committee, where he could help organize movie industry fundraising for the war effort.

His whole perspective changed, though, when Carole was killed in a plane crash while returning from selling war bonds in Indiana. She had died while actively involved in the war effort, and now Clark felt he should follow up on her original wishes and do the same. Late in July 1942, he offered his services to the Army Air Force, went through the required physical exam, and on August 11 was officially accepted and sworn in as Private Clark Gable, SN 19125741, by Col. Malcolm Andres. Clark hadn't chosen the AAF randomly; the man in charge, Lt. Gen. Henry H. "Hap" Arnold, had already let him know he had a job there waiting for him.

Clark hadn't wanted the obvious short cut that he could have taken: accepting a commission immediately. If he was going to be an officer, he typically wanted to earn both rank and respect the same way as every other enlistee. So Private Gable was promptly sent off to Officer Candidate School in Miami, Florida, for 13 weeks of hell in the heat. Hundreds of screaming women waylaid his train

57   Congratulating Clark at his graduation from Officers' Candidate School is Lt. Gen. H. "Hap" Arnold, commander of the U.S. Army Corps on October 28, 1942 (courtesy the Gable Archive).

at every major station, so much so that they caused him to miss his Florida connection at New Orleans. He finally reached Miami Beach the next day to discover that much of his army life would still be a media spectacle, from his first haircut that also involved removing the famous moustache, to trying on his new uniform, to training on the field.

Reveille was at 4:15 and there was a morning march before breakfast, then it was drills, exercises, classes, cleaning latrines and floors, and the insulting remarks from officers who were trying to wash this star recruit out. They were paraded for extended periods every day, dressed in full equipment at four in the afternoon. At this time of the year the temperature was over 100 degrees but if you fainted twice, you were out. Ambulances would circle the parade ground, picking up the unconscious. Gable stuck it out, aware that because of his public tough-guy image it would look almost as good for the OCS to wash him out, thereby proving they treated macho film stars the same as everyone else.

Then there were classes in military law, transportation, tactics and supply which were not easy for a tenth grade dropout. However, Clark's training as an actor in memorizing lines came in handy. At night he would retire to the rest rooms where the lights were on and

58 In this photograph taken by Lutrelle Conger, Clark is smartly at attention on final parade at OCS Miami in October 1942 (with permission from Linda Thompson).

study for hours to pass tests. His system worked. Clark graduated among the top third of his 2599 classmates of 42-E on October 28, 1942. He took the oath as they did, accepting his commission as Second Lieutenant Gable, 0565390. By then, he was so well-liked and accepted by his colleagues that they asked him to give the class response to Gen. Arnold's graduation address.

58–59 According to Lutrelle's daughter, Linda Thompson, her mother heard from her brother-in-law that Clark would be at a particular Miami Beach hotel for the graduation party. So, because they naturally wanted to see Clark, her brother-in-law took Lutrelle and a friend of hers over to the hotel and dropped them off. As the party was in full swing by then with lots of people going in and out, they plucked up their courage and just walked right in like they were invited guests. Soon the strikingly beautiful Lutrelle attracted Clark's attention and she was invited to sit with him at his table, and later they danced. Lutrelle knew Clark and his classmates were leaving the OCS base the next day and that there would be a final parade. Perhaps it had been published in the newspaper. So she was right there to take a couple of pictures of him in uniform with his classmates as they went by, and this is one of them.

Before Clark could enter active service, though, there was the small matter of gunnery practice. Clark proceeded to Tyndall Field, near Panama City, for an activity he at last knew

59 Enjoying the sun on Miami Beach in 1942 are (from right to left): Lutrelle Conger, her friend Eleanor Clancy and her sister Inez Conger Skelton (with permission from Linda Thompson).

something about—firing guns. He grew his moustache back, had his uniforms tailored and looked every inch the successful officer. He trained in aircraft identification and in rifle, turret gun and machine gun maintenance and firing. Finally he had gunnery practice while flying in a plane. On January 6, 1943, he graduated from gunnery school and was awarded his silver wings as a first lieutenant by Col. W. A. Maxwell, who declared Clark had been an excellent student. Clark said he'd enjoyed the training program with a fine group of men who had "blood in their eyes" and wanted to see action. From there he was posted to Fort George Wright in Spokane, Washington, where the Second Air Force trained and organized bomber crews for combat duty. On January 28, he was assigned to 508 Squadron of Col. William Hatcher's 351st Heavy Bombardment Group of the Eighth Air Force's First Air Division, based at Pueblo, Colorado.

60 Clark flew in, fought in and filmed from B-17 bombers. By modern standards a four-engine B-17 was not a large airplane, only 74 feet long with a wingspan of 103 feet. Flying flat out with empty bomb racks, its maximum speed was around 300 miles an hour. With a full bomb load, full fuel tanks and its crew of 10 on board (pilot, co-pilot, bombardier, navigator and six gunners, of whom two doubled as engineer and radio operator), speed was reduced to around 200 miles an hour at a cruising altitude of 20 to 25,000 feet. Needless to say, there was little space to spare inside; waist gunners stood back to back and practically beside one another. There was no room in the turrets or tail-gunner's positions for parachutes; they were stored in the fuselage.

The B-17 had been christened the Flying Fortress because of its heavy armament of .50 and .30 caliber guns. Nevertheless, the Luftwaffe quickly became aware of two critical weaknesses in the bomber's defenses: they originally had no nose guns and thus could be attacked head-on, and they tended to catch fire easily when hit because of the large quantity of ammunition and fuel they carried. Improvements were made and deficiencies rectified during World War II, though, and nearly 13,000 B-17s of various models eventually saw service in every theater of the conflict.

60 A side view of a typical B-17, *Chatterbox* (42-31899), from the 510 Squadron, 351 Bomber Group, U.S. Eighth Air Force, based at Polebrook, U.K. *Chatterbox* went down in Switzerland, May 1944, and the crew were interned (courtesy Ken Harbour, 351st BG Memorial Association).

61 Photographed (in April 1943) not long after he'd climbed out of his bomber on arrival at Polebrook Air Base in England, a rumpled Clark looks pretty much like any plane passenger after a really long flight (courtesy Ken Harbour, 351st BG Memorial Assoc).

61–62 Despite considerable initial skepticism that Clark would ever engage in anything that even faintly resembled actual combat, he surprised everyone by doing just that. Because of the difficulties of recruiting gunners for bomber crews at that time, probably because of the diminishing chances of them surviving an entire tour alive, he had been given the seemingly innocuous job of producing a training film that would show the typical daily activities of a heavy bomber group and feature interviews with crew members. The War Office probably figured that this little project would keep Clark happily amused and out of harm's way. Before they left the U.S., Clark insisted that prolific scriptwriter John Lee Mahin, with whom he had worked on a number of films, be added to the film crew.

However, the War Office didn't take into account Clark's strong sense of duty combined with perhaps a certain lack of concern about his personal safety; he was still somewhat depressed over Carole's death. Within days of his mid–April arrival with the 351st Bomb Group at the Polebrook Air Base, about 80 miles north of London, Clark was on board a bomber over Europe, getting shot at.

While they had been waiting for the 351st to become fully operational, some senior

62   Clark and the crew of the *Eight Ball MKII*, 303rd Bomb Group (Heavy), U.S. Eighth Air Force, after their return from mission #33 to Antwerp on May 4, 1943. From left to right, Sgt. William Mulgrew, Sgt. Richard Fortunak, T/Sgt. Roman Zaorski, Sgt. Murel Murphy, Lt. Robert Yonkman, Lt. Col. William Hatcher (mission co-pilot), Capt. William Calhoun, Jr. (pilot), Lt. Joseph Strickland, T/Sgt. Charles Terry, S/Sgt. Willard Stevens, and Capt. Clark Gable (courtesy www.303rdBG.com).

rofficers, including Clark, flew out of nearby Molesworth Air Base on familiarization flights with crews of the 303rd Heavy Bomb Group, known as the Hells Angels. Activated in February 1942 at Gowen Field, Boise, Idaho, the 303rd had arrived in England in September and October of that year and so were already seasoned veterans with much mission experience they could share with the newcomers. In January 1945, they would become the first heavy bomb group to complete 300 missions from an American air base in England. Clark flew his first mission on May 4, 1943, with the 359th Squadron's B-17 bomber *8 Ball Mk II* piloted by Capt. William R. Calhoun, Jr., to bomb the Ford and General Motors plants at Antwerp in Belgium, the 303rd's 33rd mission. Col. William Hatcher, who would be commanding officer of the 351st BG at Polebrook, was in the co-pilot's seat on his second mission.

    Although Clark flew on only a few missions, he didn't go on "milk runs." Sometimes taking a camera with him, he usually crewed as a waist gunner. The only position with worse casualty statistics was the ball gunner's turret underneath a B-17, so Clark was in real danger every time he went up. Shells went right through the fuselage in close proximity to him on multiple missions, beginning with this first one. Some 27 crews from the 303rd flew to Antwerp on this occasion along with those from the 305th and the 91st Groups. Even though the bombers were escorted and the flak light, the fighter attacks were persistent and close. Some pilots and crew thought they were going to be rammed by enemy fighters. Lt. Joseph Strickland, navigator on the *Eight Ball Mk II*, reported that a 20mm shell cut his flying boot almost in half. Clark manned the radio room .50 caliber gun and helped keep the damage to the bomber to a minimum. When

they saw that he was prepared to take the same risks and face the same dangers as they did, his fellow fliers readily accepted Clark as one of them, commenting later that "Gable is a real guy and means business." Clark just said that he'd learned a lot.

During their three years at Polebrook, between April 1943 and June 1945, the 279 B-17s of the 351st flew 311 credited combat missions during which they destroyed 303 enemy aircraft. Incidentally, the commander of 508 Squadron from May 1943 to August 1945 was Lt. Col. James T. Stewart. That's right, *that* Jimmy Stewart.

The *8 Ball Mk II* would win renown not just for its asso-

63 While visiting Oundle School, near the Polebrook base, Clark chats with sports master Frank Spragg in 1943 (photograph by Graham Priestman reproduced with kind permission of Oundle School Archive).

64 Andrew Mcintyre, cameraman for the *Combat America* film crew, shooting scenes of the Oundle School cricket team in action. Scriptwriter John Lee Mahin is on the extreme right (photograph by Graham Priestman reproduced with kind permission of Oundle School Archive).

ciation with Clark but as the lucky lead ship that always returned. It completed 37 missions until it was scrapped in New Mexico in August 1945.

63–65   The closest town to Polebrook and its air field, built for the RAF in 1940, was the ancient market town of Oundle which was only a little over three miles away. Clark enjoyed driving over there whenever he could during his stay in 1943 and, given his soft spot for children, he never passed up a chance to visit the Oundle School.

One of the oldest surviving public schools in the U.K., Oundle School was originally established for local boys in 1556 by Sir William Laxton, who had been Lord Mayor of London during the reign of Henry VIII. Maintained and operated by the Worshipful Company of Grocers, the school had a reputation which had grown so much by the mid–19th century that in 1876 it was divided into Laxton Grammar for the boys from the town and surrounding villages, and Oundle School for the sons of gentlemen from further afield. By 1922, Oundle School was the leading education facility for science and engineering within the English independent school system. It became co-educational in 1990 and 10 years later the two schools reunited to become the one current facility with a population of about 1000 students, the third largest independent boarding school in England.

It took the people of Oundle a while to become accustomed to seeing a famous Hollywood personality strolling down the High Street, but to their surprise they found Clark affable and obliging. He would stop and chat with the townsfolk, sign autographs for the schoolboys, and would often keep up his gun skills with a few shots at marauding rooks on local farmland. He could be seen touring around on his motorcycle, drinking in local pubs such as the Kings Arms and The Rose and Crown, and he became a keen softball player. Clark even showed an interest in cricket techniques, though no one actually recalls him standing at the wicket. On the whole, he was remembered later as a quiet and retiring man who preferred to melt into the background rather than be given special treatment.

65   Some eager young fans collect Clark's autograph at Oundle School (photograph by Graham Priestman reproduced with kind permission of Oundle School Archive).

66 Clark and some of his *Combat America* film crew photographed taking a break at Molesworth Air Base. Captain William Calhoun, pilot of the *8 Ball Mk II*, is on the right. Seated next to Clark is John Lee Mahin, and Sgt. Boles is grappling with the camera tripod. Standing behind Clark is T/Sgt. Van R. White and behind Mahin is Sgt. James E. Wylde from 358th Squadron Operations (with permission from Bill Wylde).

66 As well as flying in bombers and visiting towns, hospitals and other air bases by way of some morale-boosting, Clark and his crew shot footage for the training film that would later become known as *Combat America*, the only movie that Clark directed. Like all of his work, Clark treated this job professionally, rising at seven in the morning to be off in his Jeep to the day's assignment by 8:30, seven days a week when they were in the middle of a shooting schedule. They were often on the road touring airfields where they interviewed and filmed returned bomber crews and wounded personnel.

There were five in the film crew: Capt. Andrew McIntyre, first cameraman; Lt. Howard Voss, sound; M/Sgt. Merlin (or Marlin) Toti, film assistant; M/Sgt. Robert Boles, camera operator, and Capt. John Lee Mahin, scriptwriter. Howard Voss would continue a post–war career as a sound engineer for such movies as *Westward the Women* (1951) and *North by North-west* (1959). Along with Clark and McIntyre, Robert Boles later received an Air Medal for his work behind the camera, often carried out under life-threatening conditions.

67 Lt. Col. William R. (Bill) Calhoun, Jr., as he eventually became, was the pilot of *8 Ball MkII* (#41-24635) and a feature personality in *Combat America*. During World War II he flew 38 combat missions, some of them as the 359th Squadron's commanding officer and as a director of operations and executive officer. As well as 20 missions in *8 Ball Mk II*, he flew six in the original *8 Ball* that was written off after a wheels-up crash-landing by Calhoun who had ordered the rest of the crew to bail out) and various missions in six other B-17F bombers.

Born in Birmingham, Alabama, Calhoun had a degree from Sanford University and was in his early twenties when this photograph was taken. He'd arrived at Molesworth in October 1942, and by the time he met Clark the following year he was the 359th Squadron's commanding officer. In August, he completed his first 25 mission combat tour and then volunteered for a second. He was awarded two Silver Stars and the Croix de Guerre. When Calhoun was promoted to lieutenant colonel, Gable himself pinned on the insignia.

Calhoun continued flying after the war, and in 1948 he piloted the successful night-time ditching of a C-54 transport in the Pacific between Kwajalein and Hawaii with the eventual loss of only three lives. Thirty-four crew and passengers survived after spending 40 hours in the water taking turns to rest in their two five-man life rafts. Calhoun later commented in typically understated manner that they didn't ditch; they just ran out of altitude. He eventually worked for General Dynamics as a program manager for the F-111. Tragically, his only son was killed in a motorcycle accident. Bill was a man of kindness, generosity and wisdom, a very interesting man with many harrowing stories of his service with the 303rd. He always said he had a wonderful time with Clark, whom he remembered as a true gentleman with lots of class; when they went to London on leave together, Bill consequently never lacked for attention from the ladies. He passed away in 1991 in Fort Worth, Texas.

67 Capt. William R. Calhoun, Jr., John Lee Mahin and Clark are still taking that cigarette break (with permission from Bill Wylde).

68 Designed by William Mangnall, the magnificent 75-bedroom Birkdale Palace Hotel was built in 1866 at a cost of £60,000 on a site fronting the Birkdale shore. A 200-meter promenade along the seafront allowed guests to take full advantage of the view. In 1881 it was refurbished as a hydropathic establishment with outdoor facilities for archery, bowling and croquet plus riding stables. After various extensions over the years, the vast structure was boasting 1000 rooms and 200 bedrooms and suites by the outbreak of World War II and was a successful family holiday resort and conference center. In 1942 it was taken over by the American Red Cross as the largest of their rest and recreation homes, popularly known by 8th Air Force personnel as "flak shacks." By the end of the war, some 15,000 of them had recuperated from active service there. After liquidation, the hotel was demolished in 1969 and the land subdivided for a housing estate.

Andrew (Andy) McIntyre had only just begun his career behind the movie camera at MGM when he found himself sent into war alongside Clark. After the war, he picked up where he had left off and was camera operator on such movies as *The Asphalt Jungle* (1950) and *King Rat*

68 Behind the Birkdale Palace Hotel, in Southport, England (in use at the time as a Red Cross R&R club for air crews), Sgt. Boles (at the camera) and Capt. Andy McIntyre shoot scenes for *Combat America* (courtesy Alvin Hulse).

(1965) before moving to television where he became director of photography for episodes of *The FBI* (1966), *The Invaders* (1968) and *Mission Impossible* (1968).

69–70 Clark and John Lee Mahin had known each other for many years before Clark insisted that Mahin write the script for his film. Mahin always wanted to be a playwright, but he was sidetracked at first by journalism, acting and copywriting. In 1931, Ben Hecht

69 Capt. John Lee Mahin, scriptwriter for *Combat America,* outside the Palace Hotel (courtesy Alvin Hulse).

70   Mahin trying for a long catch behind the Palace Hotel while taking a break from *Combat America* (courtesy Alvin Hulse).

71   Clark talking to Sgt. Philip Hulse, a crew member of the *Argonaut III*, alongside one of the guns of the *Delta Rebel 2* in June 1943 (courtesy the Gable Archive).

invited Mahin to go with him from New York to Hollywood to work on *The Unholy Garden* and then on *Scarface*. Mahin never looked back. His first screenplay was for one of Gable's early major films, *Red Dust* (1932), and he and Gable struck up a friendship with the director Victor Fleming that would last for many years. In fact, Mahin later claimed he was instrumental in getting Gable the lead role in *Red Dust*, which was originally going to be for John Gilbert. Mahin, who died in 1984, spent most of his screen career at MGM and became Clark's favorite writer, contributing to at least nine of his movies, including the 1953 *Red Dust* remake *Mogambo*. He once commented that Clark was a very gentle man with eyes that were open and frank like a child's, and that was why women liked him. However, he added, Clark was known to become irritated with a woman who made a fool of herself.

For the information about Mahin I am indebted to *Backstory: Interviews with Screenwriters of Hollywood's Golden Age* by Patrick McGilligan (University of California Press, 1986), pp. 241–65.

71–73   Clark worked with pilot Lt. Theodore Argiropoulos and the crew of the 351st Bomb Group's B-17 bomber *Argonaut III* (29851 YB-J) for many of the flight sequences of *Combat America*. He remained friends with some of them; turret gunner Philip Hulse and the ball turret gunner Kenneth Huls from Oklahoma made a number of public appearances with him. In fact Kenneth and Philip were seen so often together that they became known as the "gold dust twins." Philip Hulse, who came from Springfield, Missouri, had enlisted on June 9, 1942, and had been Clark's on-board gunnery instructor. He and Kenneth Huls had met at gunnery school in Harlingen, Texas. When they graduated they were shipped to Geiger Field at Spokane, Washington, from where they eventually joined the 351st Bomb Group at Biggs Field in El Paso, Texas.

After nine missions, the crew of the *Argonaut III* had shot down 11 enemy fighters. On their first mission (May 14, 1943), they had taken such a beating their plane was written off when they landed. Both their wing men had gone down and Provenzale had been severely wounded and hospitalized.

Theodore Argiropoulos, or "Arge" as Clark called him, came from Shasta and Redding in California. While his father's side of the family was Greek, his mother's Randall family was Native American Wintu. Having always wanted to fly, he enlisted in the Army Air Corps while in Junior College and was an original member of the 351st Bomber Group. He and Clark apparently met while still in the U.S. and struck up a friendship that resulted in Clark choosing to use Ted's bomber and its crew as the focus for his film. Ted was a very experienced pilot with some 900 hours of multi-engine flight time when he flew his first combat mission in early May 1943.

Like its predecessors, *Argonaut III* didn't survive the war. Coming home on October 10, 1943, after their 24th mission, it was attacked over Northern France by 12 twin-engine Me-210 fighter bombers carrying rockets. Ted performed some violent maneuvers to avoid rockets until six P-47s showed up and helped them shoot down the enemy planes. By the time they were over the Channel, Ted knew they would not have enough fuel to make it home. Over Norfolk at 2500 feet, he ordered everyone to wait by the forward hatch with their para-chutes on and then turned the plane to head it back out over the Channel. As Phil waited in the dark, he suddenly felt Ted tap him on the shoulder and say: "Don't you think it's time we ought to get out of here?" One by one, they stepped out into the night air. Hulse landed safely in the backyard of a house, and Ken Huls broke his leg when he cut himself loose from the tree he was hung up in, but they and the rest of the crew survived the war. (Of the 120 original members of the 508th Bomb Squadron, only 13 made it home.)

72   The crew of the *Argonaut III* early in their tour, before they were rejoined by Navigator First Lt. Peter Provenzale. Rear from left: T/Sgt. Kenneth Huls (ball turret gunner), Lt. J. Tynam, Lt. C. Shaw, Lt. Theodore Argiropoulos [Ted Randall] (pilot); Second Lt. Richard Bohney (co-pilot); T/Sgt. Philip Hulse (turret gunner). Front from left: T/Sgt. J.S. Cebunak, T/Sgt. F.P. Tock, T/Sgt. J. Pedri (radio operator) and T/Sgt. R.M. Pierson (courtesy Alvin Hulse).

Ted later changed his name to Randall and moved to Louisville, Kentucky, where he married. He and his wife Wanda later moved to North Carolina. He passed away in 2009. Ken Huls died the same year at age 89. Pete Provenzale and J.P. Pedri (whose son's godfather was Frank Sinatra) have likewise passed within the last few years.

Philip Hulse, who was awarded the DFC and Air Medal with three Oak Leaf Clusters, is the last surviving member of the crew. In July 1945, while in Los Angeles for his service discharge, Phil was stopped at an intersection in a car with his second tour navigator, Rodney Hibler, when who should pull up alongside on a motorcycle but Clark. Phil jumped out of the car and he and Clark embraced in the middle of the street, and then all three men celebrated for the rest of the day. Not wanting anyone to think he received any special treatment, Phil had never mentioned to any of his fellow crew that he had once been in a movie with Clark Gable.

73 Lt. John Lee Mahin, T/Sgt. Philip Hulse, M/Sgt. Robert Boles, T/Sgt. Kenneth Huls, and Lt. McIntyre gathered around a military transport. Their leather A-2 jackets have the 508th Squadron patch (courtesy Alvin Hulse).

74 Like so many other bombers, *Delta Rebel 2* didn't survive the war but it certainly became one of the more famous B-17 bombers due to the circulation of various photographs and film footage of Clark standing alongside it. There is also footage of Clark shooting the bomber's .50 caliber waist gun while on the ground, taken while Gable and his film crew were involved in a press conference at Bassingbourne on June 5, 1943.

Delta Rebel 2 was one of the original nine bombers that formed the 323rd Squadron, and for the duration of its first tour, the pilot was Lt. George Birdsong, along with Lt. Chuck Bennett, co-pilot; B.Z. Byrd, radio operator; Randy Peterson, left waist gunner; Steve Perri, ball turret gunner; Harry Kulchesky, right waist gunner; Robert Abb, bombardier; and Robert Card, tail gunner. Thanks to Birdsong's early insight into a classic defense weakness of the B-17F, *Delta Rebel 2* was one of the first to have

74 Studying its artwork of a Confederate colonel, Clark stands by the nose of *Delta Rebel 2*, stationed at Bassingbourne with the 323rd Squadron of the 91st Bomber Group (courtesy www.303rdBG.com).

a .50 caliber machine gun fitted to the nose, courtesy of the squadron sheet-metal fitters and welders. *Delta Rebel 2* was also well-known because of claims that it, and not the equally famous *Memphis Belle*, was the first B-17 to complete 25 missions over Europe. That achievement, however, was probably a close thing amongst a number of aircraft in the 91st Group.

Its nose art of the Confederate colonel is considered to be the work of Corporal Tony Starcer, a famous bomber nose artist from the 91st responsible for work on over 122 planes including such well-known art as *Memphis Belle, Miami Clipper, Pist'l Packin' Mama, Rhapsody in Red* and *Shoo Shoo Baby.* Originally assigned to painting official markings on bombers, Starcer soon displayed a talent for more pictorial designations that quickly became famous throughout the British bases. Using his own recipe of ordinary house paint thinned with linseed oil, he could create flesh tones and images in a day or less that amazed everyone who saw them. Then he would paint smaller versions on the A-2 jackets of the crew. After the war, Starcer gave up painting until the 1970s, when interest in wartime nose art began to develop to such an extent that he was persuaded to begin painting versions of his previous work. When *Shoo Shoo Baby* was restored in 1981, Starcer came along to repair his original painting.

75   Amongst a number of achievements, Steve Perri has two rare distinctions: He survived 25 missions as a B-17 ball turret gunner, and 23 of them were with the *Delta Rebel 2.* In recognition of that service and the four fighters he was credited with destroying, he received the Air Medal and three Oak Leaf Clusters with his Distinguished Flying Cross. His service was not without narrow escapes; on one occasion, Birdsong had to land with only two working engines, a wounded co-pilot and two wounded crew, a load of bombs and no brakes. They went off the end of the runway, across a road, over a ditch, between two telegraph poles and into a haystack — and stopped safely.

75   Clark changing into his coat that has just been handed him by Steve Perri (partially visible on the right), the ball turret gunner of *Delta Rebel 2,* in June 1943 (courtesy the Gable Archive).

After Birdsong and his crew had completed their tour, *Delta Rebel 2* continued on under the command of Second Lt. Robert Thompson until it was shot down over Germany during the mission to Gelsenkirchen on August 12, 1943, its 33rd mission over enemy territory. Six crew members survived.

76   Clark is about to depart with the crew of *Jennie* on his first combat mission with the 351st Bomb Group. The target was Villacoublay in France, but the cloud cover was too dense and they returned without bombing it.

From Eunice, Louisiana, Ledoux was the 509th Squad-

76 Clark (third from right) with some of the crew of *Jennie* (42-29948) on June 26, 1943. Pilot Lt. Col. William Hatcher is second from right and co-pilot Maj. Elzia Ledoux is far left (courtesy Robert F. Dorr Collection).

ron Commander from November 1942, to July 1944. He had signed up as a cadet in 1940 while still in college before the U.S. entered the war. Eventually awarded the Air Medal with five Oak Leaf Clusters, the Silver Star and the Distinguished Flying Cross, Ledoux would be renowned for his attempt to guide the disabled *Ten Horsepower* in to land at Polebrook and Molesworth while flying alongside in *Q-Queenie* (*My Princess*). After the war, Col. Ledoux commanded the 4510th Air Base Group at Luke Air Force Base, Texas. He died in July 2006.

Clark's third mission was on August 12 with Maj. Theodore "Ross" Milton and Capt. John B. Carraway and crew aboard *Aint It Gruesome* to bomb the synthetic oil refinery at Gelsenkirchen in the Ruhr Valley, otherwise known as "Happy Valley." This was the first heavy daylight bombing raid to the heart of the Ruhr. Over the target at 27,000 feet, cloud cover and smoke as well as the heaviest flak yet encountered made accurate bombing of the target impossible, and so they were diverted to bomb the secondary target of the Vereinigte Stahlwerke steel mill at Bochum. This was undoubtedly Clark's most dangerous mission so far; as they turned away from the target, they became involved in running gunfights with well over 100 German fighters. Of the 243 attacking aircraft that included Clark's buddies Maj. Calhoun and the crew of the *Eight Ball Mk II*, 25 were lost. Eleven of the 351st Group's planes were severely damaged, one so badly it crash-landed on returning. *Aint It Gruesome* was attacked at least five times by fighters; one 20mm shell came up through the deck, cut off the heel of Clark's boot and exited only a foot from his head. After they landed, the crew counted 15 holes in the bomber. Lt. James Nix, co-pilot of the *Eight Ball Mk II*, accurately and succinctly described it as "a shaky do." Six months later, on February 11, 1944, the luck of *Aint It Gruesome*, later renamed *Kentucky Babe*, ran out when it was shot down on a mission to Frankfurt.

By then, on September 9, Clark had flown his fourth mission (on September 9) to the Lille-Nord Aerodrome with the 509th Squadron's *Major Ball* (42-29825), piloted by Lt. Col. Robert Burns and co-piloted by Maj. Elzia Ledoux. A number of bombers in the 351st BG had the word "ball" in their name, said to be in honor of Maj. Clinton Ball, the 511th Squadron's commander from November 1942 to September 1943. Six days later, piloted by Capt. James T. Stewart, *Major Ball* crash-landed short of the Polebrook runway on its return from a mission to Romilly.

Clark's last mission, on September 23, was an early morning strike against German naval installations in the port area of Nantes, France. He flew with Lt. Col. Burns, the 510th Bomb Squadron commander Maj. John Blaylock, co-pilot Lt. Col. John B. Carraway (who would command 511th Squadron from October 1943 to August 1945) and the crew aboard the lead bomber *The Duchess* (42-29925) of the 510th Squadron. The weather was bad, the flak accurate, and the German fighter attacks were so severe that Clark manned a nose gun for a large part of the trip. Fifty fighters intercepted them 30 minutes out from the target and followed them all the way in. By the time they landed, *The Duchess* was liberally punctured with shell holes.

On October 4, Clark was awarded the Air Medal which all airmen received after completing five missions. The very real hazards ever-present during Clark's service were emphasized on December 31 when the lead B-17, 42-37731, being flown on a bombing mission by Col. Hatcher and Maj. Blaylock, was shot down over Cognac. Blaylock was killed and Hatcher captured. *Jennie*, the first 351st bomber in which Clark had flown, did not return from the same mission.

77　　Born about two weeks before Clark, Phyllis Virginia "Bebe" Daniels (1901–1971) was one of that small, select group of movie stars who made the successful transition from silent movies to talkies, radio and then TV. Beginning her acting career at the age of four, she starred as the first Dorothy in the 1910 *The Wonderful Wizard of Oz*. As a teenager, she approached Hal Roach and Harold Lloyd and quickly became their leading lady in scores of comedy shorts. By the 1920s, Bebe was under contract with Paramount and playing opposite Rudolph Valentino. She was picked up by RKO with the advent of sound where she starred in a number of musicals during 1930. The following year she moved to Warner Brothers where, amongst others, she appeared in the 1931 version of *The Maltese Falcon*, in *Silver Dollar* (1932) and in probably her most well-known role: the fading Broadway star Dorothy Brock in the highly successful *42nd Street* (1933).

After her 1930 marriage to actor Ben Lyon, Bebe eventually retired from movies and the family moved to London where they worked in BBC radio shows. For many years Lyon and Daniels starred in the long-running radio show *Hi Gang*, for which Daniels wrote much of the dialogue. It became hugely popular during World War II. Daniels was subsequently awarded the Presidential Medal of Freedom by Harry S Truman for her service. After the war, the entire Lyon family starred in the radio sitcom *Life with the Lyons* which eventually made the transition to television.

77   Clark broadcasting from England on the BBC radio program "Stars and Stripes" on June 6, 1943, with (from left) Sgt. Roscoe Grisham, Bebe Daniels, and Sgt. Kenneth Huls from the *Argonaut III* (courtesy the Gable Archive).

78   Arriving back in Pasadena, California, on November 1, 1943, Clark is met at the railroad station by his executive assistant Jean Garceau, Ralph Wheelwright and Howard Strickling (courtesy Carole Sampeck/Carole Lombard Archive).

78–79 By mid–October 1943, Clark and his film crew had shot over 50,000 feet of color film and were ready to bring it and themselves back to the United States. Clark received his orders to fly direct to Washington, D.C., and report to the Pentagon, while the film and equipment came back by boat. He found himself on a C-47 heading back to the U.S. along with members of the crew of *Argonaut III* who had just survived their 25th mission, the horrendous second attack on Schweinfurt that cost 20 percent of the bomber force. When he arrived in Washington to report to the War Office, hundreds of female clerks and stenographers jammed the Pentagon corridors while a rather embarrassed Clark had to take part in a huge press conference in front of 100 reporters, very much aware that men had sacrificed their lives during combat in planes alongside him whereas he had survived and come home.

Finally they let him board a train for California, and he stepped off the train at Pasadena to the cheers of 300 waiting people along with a bevy of cameramen and reporters. Howard Strickling had sent the studio car to pick up Clark's personal assistant, Jean Garceau, and she joined him and Ralph Wheelwright at the station. As you can see in the photo, Clark was in uniform and wearing his campaign ribbons. Jean thought he looked much thinner than when she had least seen him, and there was noticeable gray at his temples now. They all retired to the ranch at Encino for a gathering of friends and a welcome home party. On his first appearance in the MGM studio commissary for lunch a few days later, everyone in the room stood and broke into spontaneous and thunderous applause.

Howard Strickling (1896–1982), on the right in this photo, had started as a publicist at the Metro studio in 1919 and eventually became the head of publicity at MGM. His time there closely paralleled that of Clark, with whom he was good friends and from whom he was seldom far away. He and MGM vice-president Eddie Mannix both had long-standing reputations as two of the great studio "fixers" who could tone down star scandals and even, in some cases, make them disappear. After all, major stars like Clark were assets worth millions to a studio; the loss of such a financial investment could potentially doom them, so they were literally prepared to do anything to prevent that. People such as Strickling and Mannix were employed as "disaster managers" to keep secrets, to control what the police might see, the press might write and what the adoring public would know.

The man next to Strickling is writer and publicist Ralph Wheelwright (1898–1971), Strickling's right-hand man in life as he is in this photograph and another friend of Clark's. He also worked with Whitey Hendry, the MGM police chief, to make sure that the press angle was covered in the case of any MGM star mishaps. From about 1938, Wheelwright turned his hand to writing and producing. When he and his wife wanted to adopt a baby girl in 1940, Edna Gladney of the Texas Children's Home and Aid Society in Fort Worth found a child for them. Inspired by Gladney's selfless devotion, Wheelwright wrote her life story and presented it to L.B. Mayer. The result was the remarkable film *Blossoms in the Dust* (1941) starring Greer Garson, Walter Pidgeon and a lot of children. He also wrote the story for *Man of a Thousand Faces* (1957), a biopic of Lon Chaney.

By January 1944, Clark's precious film footage had arrived and so Gable reported for work to Paul Mantz, now a lieutenant colonel, at "Fort Roach," the headquarters for the photographic division of the Air Corps at the Hal Roach Studios in Culver City. Most of the cutting and editing on that 50,000 feet of celluloid, however, was actually carried out at MGM by John Lee Mahin and editor Blanche Sewell. The end result was the creation of four Air Force training films and one major promotional film, *Combat America*. It was intended for general theatre release to boost morale for the war effort, but when the Office of War Information saw the final version their opinion was that it resembled William Wyler's 1944 documentary *The Memphis*

Belle too closely. Not only that, they claimed, a critical shortage of film stock now prevented the film being printed in 35mm format for general release to theatres. The real reason for limiting *Combat America*'s release, though, may well have been the film's unglamorous, over-the-shoulder, grainy realism. While it might look different to current "reality" documentary style, to audiences at that time it was quite a hard-nosed approach to what the war in the air was really all about. It pulls no punches, showing the day-to-day life of bomber crews, interviews with wounded men, and live combat footage of bombers under attack and being shot down. Some of the men in the film confirmed later that as far as they were concerned, the film really did come to grips with the war from their combat perspective, rather than the patriotic glamorization that the OWI preferred for its potential audiences. A little later, John Huston ran into a similar conflict with the OWI over their reluctance to release his 1946 film *Let There Be Light*, about the care and repatriation of shell-shocked and traumatized soldiers.

After its first public preview in Hollywood on November 14, 1944, 200 Technicolor prints of *Combat America* were

79 Clark photographed with two unidentified Red Cross nurses by one of their friends (courtesy the Gable Archive).

eventually successfully released in 16mm format as a training film and for showing in associations, clubs, church halls and factories to promote the war effort. For the remainder of World War II, the film proved hugely popular in small venues and even eventually in some U.S. cinemas. Since then it has proved to have a remarkably long life, providing today a fascinating historical insight into the impact of World War II aerial combat and its conditions on the lives of American service personnel.

80 The keel of the ship that would become the USS *Carole Lombard* was laid down on September 10, 1943, by the California Shipbuilding Corporation at Terminal Island. In late December it was announced that Treasury Secretary Henry Morgenthau had suggested naming a Liberty ship for Carole, and she was launched with that name on January 15, 1944, in the ceremony taking place in the photo. Fifteen thousand workers and guests heard Clark speak of the importance of the Liberty ships to the war. After Irene Dunne, a close friend of Carole's, broke the traditional bottle of champagne over the ship's bow, Clark stood at attention saluting, watching with tears running down his face as the ship bearing the name of the woman he'd loved slipped away from him, just as Carole had slipped away.

Of all the Liberty ships like the *Carole Lombard* (#2557), built between September 27,

80   Irene Dunne is about to break the champagne bottle as she launches the liberty ship USS *Carole Lombard* at the Calship Yards, Wilmington, California, on January 15, 1944. At right is Louis B. Mayer of MGM, and behind her are Mrs. Walter Lang and Clark (courtesy the Gable Archive).

1941, and September 2, 1945, only a small group of 100 bore the names of women. The 2710 ships were named for eminent Americans including war correspondents and 120 heroes of the Merchant Marine, but the main stipulation was that the person for whom the ship was named had to be deceased. They were originally known as the EC2, or emergency ship, constructed to a standard mass-produced design by the U.S. Maritime Commission by some 17 shipyards to meet the urgent need for shipping generated by World War II. President Franklin Roosevelt had once referred to them as "ugly ducklings" but when launching the first of these ships, the USS *Patrick Henry*, he referred to that man's famous "Give me liberty or give me death" speech and told the audience that these ships would bring liberty to Europe. Henceforth, they were known as Liberty ships.

Each ship was 441 feet long and 56 feet wide and carried a crew of 44, along with some members of the Naval Armed Guard if the ship was armed. They could cruise at about 11 knots, and their five holds could carry some 9000 tons of cargo, plus various vehicles or airplanes or even locomotives lashed to the deck. The 250,000 parts of each ship were pre–fabricated throughout the country in 250-ton sections and welded together in assembly-line style. Eventually one could be built in an average of 42 days for about $2,000,000.

Liberty ships typically carried a mixed cargo. On her maiden voyage from Los Angeles to Calcutta, during which she weathered a huge storm, the *Carole Lombard* was laden with

REPORT OF SEPARATION

1. LAST NAME	FIRST NAME	MIDDLE INITIAL	ARMY SERIAL NUMBER	2. GRADE	3. COMPONENT
GABLE	CLARK	(NMI)	0-565390	Major	AUS

4. HOME ADDRESS AT TIME OF ENTRY INTO SERVICE	5. BRANCH OF SERVICE AT SEPARATION
	Air Corps

6. PERMANENT ADDRESS FOR MAILING PURPOSES (IF SAME AS ITEM 4, SO STATE)	7. RACE White / Negro / Other	8. U. S. CITIZEN? YES / NO
Same as Item 4	White: X	YES: X

9. ADDRESS FROM WHICH MAN WILL SEEK EMPLOYMENT (IF SAME AS ITEM 4 OR 6, SO STATE)	10. EDUCATION (IN YEARS) GRAMMAR / HIGH SCHOOL / COLLEGE
Same as Item 4	GRAMMAR: X HIGH SCHOOL: Grad.

11. SELECTIVE SERVICE DATA	REGISTERED YES / NO	LOCAL SELECTIVE SERVICE BOARD NO.	COUNTY and STATE	SEL. SERV. ORDER NO.	12. IS JOB AID DESIRED YES / NO
	YES: X	146	18451 Sherman Way, Resida, Calif.	(?)	NO: X

13. CIVILIAN OCCUPATION	14. MILITARY OCCUPATION	15. SPEC. SERIAL NO.	16. FOREIGN SERVICE WORLD WAR II YES / NO
Motion Picture Actor	Motion Picture Photo-Gunner	8537	NO: X

17. MARITAL STATUS SINGLE / MARRIED	18. NO. OF DEPENDENTS	19. PLACE OF BIRTH	20. DATE OF BIRTH	DO NOT USE THIS COLUMN
SINGLE: X		Ohio	1 Feb 1901	2. Gr. / 3. Comp.

21. MEANS OF ENTRY INTO SERVICE INDUCTION / ENLISTMENT / COMMISSION	22. PLACE OF ENTRY INTO SERVICE	23. DATE OF ENTRY INTO SERVICE	5 Branch
ENLISTMENT: X	California	7-12-42	

24. CAUSE OF SEPARATION (i.e. C.D.D., Minority, Convenience of the Gov't.)	25. PLACE OF SEPARATION	26. DATE OF SEPARATION	7 8 Race / Cit.
	Culver City, California	12 June 1944	15 M O S

27. TYPE OF DISCHARGE Honorable / Dishonorable / Other	28. CHARACTER AT SEPARATION	29. HAS PENSION CLAIM BEEN MADE YES / NO	16. F.S. / 17. Mar.
		NO: X	

INSURANCE NOTICE

IMPORTANT:—IF A PREMIUM IS NOT PAID WHEN DUE OR WITHIN THIRTY-ONE DAYS THEREAFTER INSURANCE WILL LAPSE.

Make checks or money orders payable to The Treasurer of the United States, and forward to Collections Subdivision, Veterans' Administration, Washington, D. C.

30. Kind of Insurance National Service Life Insurance / U. S. Government Life Insurance / None	(31) How Paid Allotment / Direct to V.A.	(32) Effective Date of Allotment Discontinuance	(33) Date Next Premium Should be Mailed (One Mo. After 32)	(34) Premium Due Each Month	20.Yr.B. / 21. S.
None: X					24 Cause Sep.

35. I certify that all information on this form is in accordance with the records of the War Department regarding the individual above-named and that a copy of this form informing him of his obligations under the Selective Service Law and of his rights and benefits (except where separated from the armed forces by reason of death), has been delivered to him in person.

36. *Ronald Reagan*

Signature of Organization Commander or Adjutant

RONALD REAGAN, Capt., A.C., Pers.O.

Type Name of Officer, Grade and Organization

	25 Place Sep.
	26 Date Sep.
	28 Character
	40 Med. Diag.

NOTICE TO VETERANS' ADMINISTRATION

37. It is my intention to:
(A) Continue my insurance in full [-]   (B) Continue $_____ insurance in force   (C) Discontinue my insurance [-]

NOTE:—If (c) is checked no premium notices will be sent. If reduction in insurance is desired see item 7 on reverse side of form.

	4 Residence
	10 Ed. Level
	13 Civ. Occup.

39. If discharged for physical disability, state physical limitations, if known

| | 19 Nativity |

40. If discharged for a physical or mental cause, copy sufficient data from page 2 W. D., A. G. O. Form No. 40 to clearly indicate the cause

| | 22 Place Entry |
| | 23 Date Entry |

41. If discharged for the convenience of the Gov't or transferred to the reserve, state circumstances

Transferred to Inactive Status.

W. D., A. G. O. Form No. 53
1 August 1943
(See AR 615-360)

POSTING COPY

To: The Adjutant General's Office, Washington 25, D. C.
(Folded and inserted in the Service Record ...es of enlisted men)

81 Major Clark Gable's (0-565390) Air Corps separation papers, signed on June 12, 1944, by Captain Ronald Reagan (courtesy Carole Sampeck/Carole Lombard Archive).

ammunition and explosives as well as pipe sections for the war-time oil pipelines being built in India. Just like her namesake, the *Carole Lombard* carried out missions of mercy during her life. At the beginning of April 1944, while sailing from Colombo to Fremantle, she rescued six lifeboats of survivors in the Indian Ocean from the torpedoed 6589-ton British merchant ship *City of Adelaide*, sunk on March 30 by the Japanese submarine I-8. That crew was luckier than they knew; a little over three months later, the crew of the I-8 was responsible for the on-board imprisonment and massacre of most of the men from the Liberty ship *Jean Nicolet*.

On another voyage, when loaded to capacity with high explosives, the *Carole Lombard* received an SOS from the torpedoed and sinking British freighter *Richard James Ricketts* some 1400 miles away. Sailing at full speed through rough seas frequented by submarines, the *Carole Lombard* arrived four days later at the position given by the British ship and eventually located lifeboats scattered an area of ten miles containing the entire crew of 90. For this heroic action the *Carole Lombard*'s master, Nelson M. Amy, was awarded the Meritorious Service Medal in 1946. The ship continued sailing for some years after the war until she was eventually scrapped in 1959. Two Liberty ships, the *Jeremiah O'Brien* in San Francisco and the *John W. Brown* in Baltimore, still survive today as public museum ships.

81   After these papers were signed, Clark was officially a civilian actor once again. However, in this brave, new, post-war world MGM didn't seem to know quite what to do with him, and for some time Clark didn't seem to know quite what to do with himself. After what he'd been through and seen, Hollywood concerns must have felt somewhat trivial. Many familiar faces had gone, too, and those who were now stars had been only children in the 1930s. MGM had grown bigger, but as the years went by Clark did not find it a better place to be.

Recreational Life

82–83 Contrary to what is often said, Clark didn't have to learn how to ride a horse for the movies; he already knew how to ride from his time on the farm as a teenager in Ohio. However, he did need to be taught how to ride trained movie horses as a cowboy, a different technique altogether, and as part of that he would have been taught to sit correctly in a Western saddle. Most of his previous experience had been riding bareback. Clark loved horses and treated them well, was renowned for his frequent attendance of racetracks, played a bit of polo, rode for pleasure as well as work, and owned more than one horse during his life. In late 1935, he owned a well-known filly named Beverly Hills that ran at Santa Anita and won its first race at Agua Caliente in the first two-year-old race of the season. In the fifties, in movies such as *The Tall Men* and *Across the Wide Missouri*, Clark rode Steel, a horse of which he became very fond. John Wayne can also be seen riding Steel in *Tall in the Saddle* and the infamous *The Conqueror*.

Clark's training to ride horses in movies began with his very first speaking role, that of Rance Brett in Howard Higgin's *The Painted Desert*, for which he had to look like a cowboy born to the saddle in only two weeks. Art Wilson, a former cowboy from Montana, took Clark in hand at the Griffith Park Riding Academy and soon found that he was a gifted and fearless horseman. By the end of that two weeks, Clark could not only ride but he could do a running mount and dismount, and he could lean down out of the saddle and pick up a handkerchief from the ground while at the gallop.

Before he had his own ranch and stables, Clark liked to rise at dawn every morning so he could take a horse for a gentle canter. He always said that the only thing he liked better than horses was hunting, and vice versa. Clark and Carole rode together frequently. She gave him a saddle-bred sorrel show horse named Sonny that he adored, and he in turn gave her a palomino gelding. However, it proved to be a little too spirited and so they sold it and bought Melody, a bay polo pony, which Clark kept for many years after Carole died. Although Carole was an expert horsewoman, she gradually gave up riding after she and Clark were married because she wanted to have children and was under the impression that, somehow, riding would make that more difficult.

They both had beautiful hand-made saddles crafted by Mr. and Mrs. Val of the Valdez Riding Stables in Coldwater Canyon, who helped look after their horses. Clark became so intrigued with leather tooling that he built a small workshop, took lessons and became quite good at it.

82   A young Clark looking very debonair on horseback in the early 1930s (courtesy the Gable Archive).

84   Hunting was something Clark enjoyed as much as for the pleasure of being in the open country on a good horse as anything else. Nor was all his hunting with a rifle; Clark was just as talented at "hunting" with a camera. In fact, he came to hunting through his interest in riding, and in the mid–1930s he was right into big-game hunting in the wild, either in Arizona or four days with packhorses and guide into the mountains around Jackson Hole, Wyoming. His interest in hunting had been sparked by Buster Keaton and by Mary Astor's second husband, Dr. Franklyn Thorpe. Keaton had suggested Clark should take up fishing and hunting whenever he was tired of people. Clark had always admired Thorpe's gun collection so much he started putting together one of his own.

The upshot of it all was a hunting trip into the Sierras, and Clark was hooked. Over the years he would develop his impressive gun collection, even though he seemed to be more interested in just being in the great outdoors than killing animals. Thorpe once recalled that Clark, who was an excellent fast shot, once drew a bead on a running buck, but then put his gun down when the animal stopped, saying that he could have hit it if it hadn't looked at him.

Clark prided himself on being able to travel through the wilderness with the bare essentials: 30-06 Springfield rifle, compass, first-aid kit, field glasses, and matches in a waterproof container. Their food would be the staples of bread, beans, potatoes, and bacon. Depending on the season, they'd hunt grizzlies, mountain sheep, moose and elk, but Clark would never kill them unless they needed the meat. Once they'd found the animals, it was usually out with the camera.

83 Cutting a dashing figure once again, Clark is on horseback in a setting that looks remarkably Australian for being in California (courtesy the Gable Archive).

In 1937, just after major shooting was finished for *Parnell*, Clark made a trip into Arizona's Kaibab Forest to the foothills of Saddle Mountain with his guide, "Captain Jack" Butler, and some hounds and pack horses, to capture a mountain lion. In those days they were regarded as villainous pests that slaughtered deer, calves and horses. However, only Captain Jack was carrying a 30-30 slung in a boot at his saddle; once again, Clark just carried his camera.

Two days after the party had failed to capture one big cat, the dogs treed a mountain lion cub, about six months old. Clark brought it back as a present for Carole but, she really didn't appreciate the gift of a 75-pound, toothy, disgruntled house pet.

85–87   Clark was primarily a river and lake fisherman, mainly trout and salmon. His favorite fishing spot for many years was along the Rogue River at Grants Pass in Oregon where he would stay at the Weasku Inn owned by renowned fly-fisherman William E. "Rainbow" Gibson and his wife Peggie. Over the years Clark grew close to the Gibsons and their three daughters, Sybil, Carol and Vee Alice.

The log lodge and cabins that formed the Inn were built between 1923 and 1924 for Albert and Sarah Smith on the banks of the Rogue, downstream from the Savage Rapids Dam.

The Gibsons, frequent guests who had fallen in love with the Inn, bought it only a few years later in 1927 when the Smiths retired. The Inn rapidly became popular with Hollywood personalities, writers and politicians for its salmon and trout fishing and potential for quiet relaxation.

88   During spring and fall for much of his life, Clark could be found at the Inn challenging the river's big salmon and steelhead trout. He had such a high opinion of the food prepared by the Weasku's cook, Alice Everand, that he could typically be heard at badly catered Hollywood parties commenting that he'd rather be eating her flapjacks at the Inn.

Such was his passion for the outdoors that Clark came to define people he knew by whether they shared that love, and his best friends were the men and women who could hunt, shoot, ride and

84   At the time he was working on *Parnell*, Clark went out hunting and came back with a cougar cub as a present for Carole, who was about as happy with that idea as the cat (courtesy the Gable Archive).

85 The main lodge of the Weasku Inn, Clark's favorite fishing lodge, on the Rogue River at Grants Pass, Oregon, as it looks today (photograph courtesy Country House Inns, Grants Pass, Oregon).

86 One of the suites at the Weasku Inn (photograph courtesy Sol Visual Designs, Ashland, Oregon).

camp out with him. Carole Lombard learned to do all that with Clark, and so it was no surprise to anyone that she would go to the Rogue River with him.

Nor should it have surprised anyone that Clark retreated to the Inn for three weeks immediately after Carole's funeral. He stayed in his usual room at the top of the stairs and spent a lot of time out in the river with his rod and line. By then, "Rainbow" Gibson had passed on but Peggie and the three girls continued running the place.

Clark returned to the Inn in 1945 after the war, and soon became quite close to Carol Gibson during their many fishing and rafting journeys. Eventually he asked his "girl on the Rogue," as he liked to call her, if she would marry him but Carol declined. She was only in her early twenties, and Clark had also declared he didn't want any children. The Inn remained

88 Clark standing proudly with Peggie Gibson and his catch of the day (courtesy the Gable Archive).

Clark's favorite place to be when away from his Encino ranch, though, and he went ahead and purchased some 38 acres that included his special fishing place, the Pierce Riffle. He became such a fixture around the Inn that the Gibsons treated him like one of the family. Many people thought he was a part-owner.

87 The Inn's famous period neon sign (photograph courtesy Country House Inns, Grants Pass, Oregon).

89 Although he preferred lakes and streams, Clark also liked the occasional fishing trip off the Californian coast. During the late forties, he took up game fishing, but he still had much the same attitude to the big fish as he did to deer; he preferred to throw them back, especially if they'd put up a good fight. He actually liked to be out on that fishing boat on Balboa Bay for the same reasons as he'd gone hunting in the mountains: it got him away from phones and people.

90–93 Clark loved dogs. He owned a number of them and worked with a few in movies, the most famous probably being the St. Bernard "Buck" trained by Carl Spitz for *Call of the Wild*. Probably the one he was most often photographed with was a German short-haired pointer known as Bob, or sometimes Bobby, his favorite bird dog. Bob seemed to know what Clark was going to do before he thought of it himself and, by the time the photographs on the next page were taken, Bob had been with him on three trips to Mexico. Bob was his constant companion, often sitting at his feet under the dinner table. However, Bob and Sonny the horse didn't get along so well. Sonny was always looking to land a good kick on the dog, so Clark had to make sure he kept them away from each other, which was no easy task on a morning ride. As he grew older, Bob developed a liking for ice cream, so Clark made sure he had some every night.

Carole always loved dachshunds; her favorite was Commissioner, named after a fire commissioner in Santa Barbara whom she and Clark both knew. The story was that it basically ignored Clark until Carole died

89 *Right:* Clark looks happy with his catch of the day in California, 1934 (courtesy Carole Sampeck/Carole Lombard Archive).

and then it wouldn't be separated from him, but that could be just a romantic tale. There was Tuffy, the watchdog boxer, whose reputation was somewhat tarnished when it was found he had slept in the car with a small-time burglar one night. Then there were some cats, various hens and chickens, and a few cows.

Commissioner died while Clark was away during World War II, and so when he returned Virginia Grey and Jean Garceau bought him another female dachshund puppy that he named Rover, and then he later bought another male he called Noodles. Sylvia brought him a poodle named Ricquet to be with her small Manchester terrier Minnie, but Clark was never a small dog guy.

Bob died around 1955, and Clark missed him greatly. He bought a German wire-haired pointer named Rusty, but he never measured up to expectations as a hunting dog so Clark gave him to Bunker. Then, while visiting the Happy Valley Gun Club at Riverside, Clark saw a red cocker spaniel named Caminos Red Rocket, usually just called Red. On condition that Clark pay expenses, the club trainer and manager Ivan Brower took the dog to New York for the National Field Trials. Red won the National Championship and duly became Clark's new hunting dog, sometimes known to bring in two ducks at a time. Clark was so

90 *Left:* Clark with a handful of Chow puppies, circa 1935 (courtesy the Gable Archive).
91 *Right:* Clark with his and Carole's favorite hunting dog, the German short-haired pointer Bob, circa 1940 (courtesy the Gable Archive).

proud of him that for a while Red got to sleep in the bedroom.

94 Skeet shooting once took Clark all the way to Manitoba, Canada, to hunt ducks. During early 1935, he frequently shot clay targets at the Santa Monica Gun Club with film director and friend Jack Conway. They would often meet up with the well-known Minneapolis outdoors writer Jimmy Robinson (1897–1986), who would regularly join a group of local duck-hunters to lease an old two-bedroom farmhouse on the Delta Marsh on the shore of Lake Manitoba, about 14 miles north of Portage la Prairie and 60 miles west of Winnipeg. Robinson kept telling Clark tales of the number of ducks they would bag in a season there and invited him to come up whenever he could make it.

92 In this photograph taken by Clark, Bob is outfitted for a hunting trip (courtesy the Gable Archive).

93 Clark with Bob and one of his later dachshunds, either Rover or Noodles (courtesy the Gable Archive).

Clark was an accurate and fast skeet shooter. Along with a young Robert Stack, Clark began shooting skeet in mid–1934 and was such a natural that within six weeks he was averaging 23 per round. He wasn't up there with Stack, but he was good. Stack quickly became a top skeet shooter, winning the World 20 Gauge Championship when only 17. During his career Stack broke the world long run record with low gun and at one point was the second-best shooter in the country. The two young men learned on the range at Harry Fleischmann's Los Angeles-Santa Monica Gun Club, and Stack then taught Carole Lombard to shoot at Lake Tahoe with a trap set up on the lakeshore. He spent a lot of time with both Clark and Carole, and he always remembered Clark's humanity. Once when they were in Colusa, Cal-

94 Director Jack Conway, outdoor writer Jimmy Robinson and Clark discussing the merits of duck shooting in Canada during a break from Clark's work in the movie *San Francisco*, March 1936 (courtesy Delta Marsh History Initiative/Gordon Goldsborough).

ifornia, they stopped to buy some rubber boots before heading for the duck blinds. Clark was immediately recognized and surrounded by fans. After he'd joked with them and signed autographs he returned to his friends, and the first thing the King of Hollywood did was apologize for delaying their start.

Carole discovered she enjoyed shooting almost as much as Clark, often downing more ducks than he did when they hunted together. Clark was the kind of man who could take Carole's newfound ability in his stride without suffering from any damage to his male ego. In fact, he'd often brag to his fellow hunters about his wife's accuracy. Clark wasn't competitive about his shooting; it was just a relaxing sport he thoroughly enjoyed and he could be outdoors to do it. He even indulged in skeet shooting on the *RMS Queen Mary*, taking out honors in the on-board contest while heading for a six-week vacation in France in July of 1948.

At one time Clark, his friend Ray Holmes and Barron Hilton started their own duck club at Venice Island in Northern California's Stockton River. The place was heavily populated by ducks in those days, and he was there so frequently when he wasn't working that a rumor went around he had a clause written into his movie contracts allowing him to take the duck season off. For many years after his death, the club kept the bottle of Scotch and the glass from which Clark had his last drink there in a glass case.

Clarke continued to be interested in skeet and duck shooting all his life. He and Kathleen, also a good shot, were members of the 2000-acre Hidden Valley Gun Club near Riverside because women were permitted to shoot there.

95–96 In September 1938, Clark arrived by train at Portage La Prairie, Manitoba, to be a guest of Jimmy Robinson and the Portage Country Club (courtesy Delta Marsh History Initiative/Gordon Goldsborough).

95–103 Because Clark was a busy man, two years went by before he had an opportunity to accept Robinson's invitation to hunt ducks in Manitoba. It so happened that Grant Ilseng, the top ranking shot of 1938, met Clark one day at the Santa Monica Club just after returning from the National Skeet Tournament held that year at Tulsa, Oklahoma, where Robinson had been his roommate. Ilseng had been hearing the same stories of the marsh, and so he in turn deluged Clark with yarns of Canadian canvasbacks and mallards and reminded him of Robinson's standing invitation.

When Clark looked at his schedule he realized there would be a week-long gap before he had to begin work again in October, so in early September he wired Robinson that he was on the way by train. When Clark arrived, Robinson

97 Accompanied by a friendly dog, Clark strolls along the main street of Portage to the Leland Hotel (courtesy Delta Marsh History Initiative/Gordon Goldsborough).

98   Members of the Portage Country Club with Clark and their day's duck shooting tally outside the club (courtesy Delta Marsh History Initiative/Gordon Goldsborough).

99   The Portage Country Club building as it looks today (courtesy Delta Marsh History Initiative/Gordon Goldsborough).

100 With Jimmy Robinson, left, at his camp on the Delta Marsh, Manitoba, Canada, in September 1938 (courtesy Delta Marsh History Initiative/Gordon Goldsborough).

101 Out in a canoe on the Delta Marsh with French-Canadian guide Rod Ducharme (courtesy Delta Marsh History Initiative/Gordon Goldsborough).

informed him that the weather might be too warm for successful duck hunting, but Clark said he'd be happy just to have some time off to sit around the stove at night with friends. Typically, despite the crowds, Clark wanted to meet the local people of Portage la Prairie and so he walked down the main street, bought shells and a hunting license at the local hardware store, visited the five-and-ten to say hello to the girls behind the counter, and then he bought drinks at the Leland Hotel.

When they reached the camp, Clark met the rest of the hunting group and the two French-Canadian guides. He changed his clothes and insisted on getting out onto the marsh immediately. They set out in the canoe to find the marsh full of wildfowl. Within an hour of setting up their decoys among the rushes, Clark, using a double-barrel Parker and a Winchester pump, had bagged his limit.

After that he would be the first out of bed every morning, waking the others by cutting wood. Then, starting at dawn, they would shoot all morning before returning at noon to rest and play some ball. Clark was in excellent shape, hiking and shooting better than most men there. Robinson observed he was so tall that his feet stuck out of the end of the bunk at night.

When the week was up, a party was held for Clark and local newspaper journalists and sportsmen back at Minneapolis' Nicolet Hotel. Then Clark returned to Hollywood, which must have seemed more like another planet than usual after being out on the Delta Marsh.

104–105 When Clark finished work on *Strange Cargo* in January 1940, he and Carole decided to go on a belated shooting honeymoon to one of his favorite hideaways, the exclusive

102 *Left:* Clark waiting for those ducks to fly over the marsh dressed in his battered Berlin-leather hat, leather pants and jacket.
103 *Right:* Playing baseball back at the camp to relax (courtesy Delta Marsh History Initiative/Gordon Goldsborough).

104 Having arrived at the exclusive La Grulla Gun Club, near Ensanada, Mexico, Clark is photographed by Carole unloading the Woody wagon, January 1940 (courtesy the Gable Archive).

105 Carole, with her back to the camera, is washing down her catch after the day's shooting at La Grulla. Grouped from left to right around her are Harry and Nan Fleischmann and Clark (courtesy the Gable Archive).

106 Clark looks relaxed on the fairway at the Bahamas Country Club in Nassau in early January 1951. He is accompanied by the club professional Al Collins (left), Nassau golf champion and New York State amateur champion Tommy Goodwin (second from right), and the club's assistant pro Jimmy Patton (courtesy Bob Davies).

La Grulla Gun Club outside of Ensanada, south of the Mexico border. They drove down in Clark's new Woody wagon that he had fitted out especially for hunting trips such as this. Traveling with them were Nan and Harry Fleischmann, who were good friends with Clark and Carole. A nephew of the wealthy Max Fleischmann, the head of the Fleischmann Yeast organization, Harry was a world skeet shooting record holder and the 1936 California State Skeet Champion. He had owned and managed a number of gun clubs including the Oasis in the Salton Sea area, the Los Angeles–Santa Monica Gun Club where he taught Robert Stack to shoot, and a club at Bakersfield. Just for fun, Harry also appeared in a number of mostly uncredited bit parts in some 30 movies.

Having no luck at bagging any ducks at La Grulla after a few days there, they drove further south to another gun club before attempting to make it back to La Grulla by Clark's birthday on February 1. On the way back it began to rain and they soon found themselves bogged on a remote mountain road in the dark. There was nothing for it but to climb into their sleeping bags after a supper of lobster and birthday cake and wait till morning.

When they hadn't arrived back at La Grulla by nightfall, the phone wires to Hollywood ran hot with the story that one of its most famous couples was missing. After all, by now Clark was earning as much in 10 weeks on a movie set as the president of the United States was paid in a year! So, when the innocently oblivious Gables finally rolled into La Grulla later that morning after a truck had pulled them out of the mud patch, it was to find they had been on the front pages of newspapers and that a search party was about to set out looking for them. Typically, they just had a big laugh about it.

106 Clark was in the Bahamas for a three-week vacation with his fourth wife, Lady Sylvia Ashley, during Christmas and New Year and into early January of 1951. For some reason, a story developed that Clark only took up golf in the mid–1950s after he married Kathleen, but there are photos of Clark swinging a club dating back to the 1930s. It's highly likely that it was his second wife, Ria, who encouraged him to take it up, as she did with many of his social pursuits. In any case, golf for Clark was purely relaxation; he was never a highly competitive player but took to the course essentially to unwind and often socialize. One of his caddies in 1949 at the Bel-Air Country Club in Los Angeles was a young boy named Robert Wagner, whom he later mentored at MGM.

Clark's name is linked with many famous courses such as Cresta Verde at Corona, founded as Parkridge Country Club in 1927 by Randolph Scott; Bermuda Dunes at Palm Springs where Clark and Kathleen had a home; Breezy Point in Minnesota; Pebble Beach; Camelback in Scottsdale, Arizona, and Half Moon in Jamaica. He reputedly once lost his wedding ring on the Arizona Biltmore course in Phoenix and rewarded groundskeepers who found and returned it. In the fifties, Clark would often play while he was traveling on a film shoot; for instance, he played at the Newquay Golf Course in Cornwall in June 1952 while he was there for *Never Let Me Go.*

Writer Jonathan Carroll's uncle used to own a very prestigious men's store in Beverly Hills and knew many movie stars. He and Clark used to play golf regularly, and one day they were on a course where one of the holes ran parallel to a public road. While they were playing that hole, a car stopped nearby and the female driver asked Carroll's uncle for directions. As it happened, he didn't know the answer to her question, so he turned and repeated the question to Clark who was putting at the time with his back turned to them. After taking his shot, he turned and ambled over to the car. Leaning on the passenger's side door, he put his head in the window and gave her the information she needed. Suddenly realizing it was Clark Gable who was giving her directions, the woman fainted.

Clark's clubs are now scattered all over the world. Somehow a set has even ended up on display in the Schloss Mittersill in the Austrian Alps. I rather think that the ex–Air Force gunner might have had a wry, ghostly chuckle about that.

Fast Life

107   Often heard to comment that if his career as an actor in movies ever went bad he could go back to earning a living as a mechanic, Clark enjoyed being both at the wheel and under the hood of the many cars he owned during his life, usually large fast ones that he tended to replace every year. Most of them he owned, although he was often pressured to be seen driving some as promotion and was apparently not above promoting more than one vehicle at a time.

108–109   Clark had a long affair with Packard cars, probably owning more of them than any other single marque. They had an elegance and classic beauty which he certainly seemed to appreciate. The company was founded as the Ohio Automobile Company by mechanical engineer James Ward Packard, William Doud Packard and George Lewis Weiss in Warren, Ohio, in 1899. Apparently James was challenged by Alexander Winton to build a better horseless carriage than Winton's and proved he could. Along the way, he developed the modern steering wheel and the first production 12-cylinder engine in their 1916 Twin Six. Mind you, at an average price of $2,600, Packards didn't come cheap in those days. Impressed by their quality, wealthy Detroit investor Henry Bourne Joy helped refinance and restructure the company to become the Packard Motor Car Company in 1902, situated on a 35-acre plant site in Detroit and considered the most modern in the world. By the 1930s, along with Pierce-Arrow and Peerless cars, Packards were regarded as the epitome of luxury automobile manufacture defined by their slogan, "Ask the man who owns one."

Instead of cutting back during the Depression, Packard went ahead and built more expensive cars. Seemingly throwing caution to the winds, they announced at the Roosevelt Hotel in New York City the revival of the Packard Twin Six for 1932 with its 445-cubic inch V12 engine, single Stromberg dual-downdraft carburetor and three-speed transmission. Originally intended for an abandoned front-wheel drive Packard version, this smooth, quiet and powerful engine was designed by Cornelius Van Ranst.

All Twin Sixes were produced in the Ninth series as either Model 905 with a 142-inch wheelbase or the 906 with a 174-inch wheelbase. They came with twin side-mounted spares, white sidewalls, driving lights, and a metal trunk with fitted luggage installed on the luggage rack at the rear. Most of the Twin Six production run had factory bodies by Raymond Dietrich, but others were crafted by Brewster, Fleetwood, Judkins and Le Baron. Nevertheless, they were a limited edition: in 1932, only 304 of the Model 905 were built with 10 body style options, along with 238 of the Model 906 with 11 options, nine of which were Individual Custom. Prices ranged from $4,150 for the three-seat 905 model 578 coupe to $7,950 for the top-end Dietrich Custom Laundelet town car, and this was during the Great Depression! Typically sold in 1932 for $5,350, a rumble-seat Roadster 905 sold in 2008 for $660,000.

It might have been an early car, but the big Packard Twin Six was not slow. It could easily, if not quickly, reach speeds of 100 mph. Each vehicle came with a certificate of approval signed by the director of the Packard Proving Grounds, Charlie Vincent, and two-time Indianapolis 500 winner Tommy Milton attesting to a 250-mile run-in.

Probably only five original Twin Six coupe roadsters survive today and one of them is Clark's, owned and restored since 2007 by Thomas Moretti.

110 When Clark signed the papers for his Packard Twelve LeBaron Runabout Speedster, VIN 902067, body #176-3, style #275, he was once again in possession of a unique vehicle. Not only was the Twelve series Packard's top-of-the-line car, but only four LeBaron Runabout Speedsters were built in 1934. Yet for the film star who had everything, even that distinction wasn't enough. No sooner had he taken delivery, than Clark handed over the car to his coachbuilders of choice, Bohman and Schwartz in Pasadena, for some personal customizing.

This Speedster was a direct descendant of the Twin Six that he had previously owned. Packard changed the name to Twelve from 1933 to 1939 to more clearly convey the nature of the vast power under the hood in the shape of that 445-cubic inch V12 engine with its polished aluminum heads developing some 160 horsepower. When these big, heavy cars were moving at the 100 mph of which they were easily capable, it really felt like speed.

In more ways than one, though, these Speedsters with their big headlights mounted on flowing, flared fenders alongside those seemingly endless, squared-off hoods would be the last of their kind before Packard began streamlining. The 1106 Runabout Speedster's lightweight body incorporated a raked V-windshield behind that long hood and ended in a racy boat-tail rear, mounted on Packard's shortest-wheelbase chassis of 134 ⅞ inches. It was actually the same chassis used for their eight-cylinder line with the same front and rear axles, wheels, brakes

107 An advertising promotion for the 1937 Dodge convertible coupe featuring Clark (courtesy the Gable Archive).

108   Clark looking very happy behind the wheel of his 1932 Packard Twin Six registered 1Y1 and featuring the goddess of speed hood ornament (courtesy the Gable Archive).

109   Thomas Moretti's restored 1932 Gable Packard Twin Six photographed at Pebble Beach in 2009 (with permission from Thomas Moretti).

110 The restored 1934 Packard Twelve, model 1106 Runabout Speedster by LeBaron once owned by Clark, now part of The Bahre Collection (courtesy The Bahre Collection, photograph Jeff Orwig).

and transmission. Pontoon fenders with rear skirts and wheel covers created a more distinctively "modern" look than production Packards of the same year.

LeBaron Carrossiers Inc. (to give them their full name) was founded in New York in 1920 by Thomas L. Hibbard and Raymond Dietrich, two of the most respected coachbuilders of their day, after they had been fired by their employer Brewster for spending too much time on their own designs. They chose the LeBaron name because it sounded French and classy. Unlike other coachbuilders, though, they initially chose to carry out purely design work without having their own workshop. In 1923, Hibbard met and decided to join "Dutch" Darrin while overseas in Paris, and he was replaced at LeBaron by Ralph Roberts. LeBaron expanded rapidly, eventually partnering with Edsel Ford to design bodies for Lincoln chassis. This led to Dietrich leaving LeBaron to join Murray Body to form his own company. Eventually LeBaron was acquired by Briggs, one of Detroit's largest body builders, where they eventually became the in-house design label, producing some of their best work on the crest of the demand for custom coach-built bodies during the twenties and early thirties. LeBaron bodies were the most frequent for the Model J Duesenbergs, for example, amongst others. By 1934, they were established designers with a reputation amongst the cream of American society for style.

Bohman and Schwartz's upgrading of the already-sleek styling of this Speedster was sparse and subtle. The standard running boards were replaced with tear-drop step plates, the windshield height was reduced by several inches and a newly created top that fitted closer with the enhanced body curves, thus creating a leaner, sleeker appearance. One of the drawbacks that even B&S couldn't correct, however, was the size of the trunk; it was about big enough for a large bag of groceries.

Each of the four 1934 Speedsters differed slightly from the other, and each had their own individual job number. Clark's Speedster was #176-3, identifying it as the second-to-last one built. The standard price for a Speedster that year was $7,746, making it the most expensive Packard money could buy off the factory floor. For many years, one of the other three Speedsters belonged to George Hormel, founder of Hormel Foods and Spam. It remained within the family until 1961, whereupon it passed through various collections before selling in 2006 for a little over $3,000,000. Another Speedster was with the same owner since 1947 and was acquired by an Ohio collector in 2008, and a third is part of a collection in Nevada.

Clark's Speedster also passed through various hands until it entered the collection of Gene Zimmerman, the owner of Automobilarama in Pennsylvania. In the late 1970s it was acquired from Zimmerman by The Bahre Collection, where it remains today having been completely restored.

111 No custom Bohman and Schwartz bodywork appears on this car. This is the same Packard 120 convertible coupe that any non–Hollywood star could walk into their local dealer and order for a little over $1,000.

111 As unusual as it may seem, Clark is photographed here in 1937 with a Packard straight from the dealer's floor: a standard 120 convertible coupe (courtesy the Gable Archive).

112   Clark's 1938 Packard Eight Convertible Victoria with coachwork by Darrin of Paris, photographed in West Hollywood in 2009 (copyright © 2009 Bonhams & Butterfields Autioneers Corp. All rights reserved).

113   The interior of the 1938 Packard convertible Victoria (copyright © 2009 Bonhams & Butterfields Autioneers Corp. All rights reserved).

As the name suggests, the 120 was named after the 120-inch wheelbase chassis. Because of financial reasons and the need to stay competitive as the Depression wreaked havoc on luxury car sales, Packard moved into the mid-priced eight-cylinder engine bracket and this car was their flagship. Produced from 1935 to 1937 and again from 1939 to 1941, it was designed and produced quickly and readily in a wide variety of soft-top and hard-top models in two-door and four-door configurations, and the smooth-running and durable eight cylinders under the hood could produce 110 horsepower. The car proved immediately successful.

The following year, while keeping the price down, Packard increased the engine to 282 cubic inches producing 120 horsepower, which could take the 120 over 85 mph; the most expensive of the line was the four-door sedan at $1,395. Then in 1937, for the first time in 10 years, they offered a Six which enabled them to move the 120 further up-market and present it with more amenities and options. Still, compared to previous Packard vehicles such as Clark's 1934 Speedster, the price of a 120 was kept low; even the limousine body style on the 138-inch wheelbase set the buyer back only $2000. Consequently, the 120 series remained popular and over 50,000 were produced that year.

112–113 Of all the Packards that Clark owned, this Convertible Victoria was both the most famous and the one he had for the shortest period — probably barely a month. A Convertible Victoria, by the way, is the name given to an open body with seating for four or five in which the top, instead of completely disappearing within the body when stowed, rests in an intermediate position behind the rear seats. It was a very distinctive custom-built vehicle, but that in itself was the problem; it was entirely too distinctive. Only the second Packard Convertible Victoria built by Darrin and the first five-seater, it may just as well have had "Clark Gable" in gold letters on the doors and therein, as Shakespeare would have said, lay the rub.

Howard A. "Dutch" Darrin was the ideal man to be a car designer for the Hollywood stars. A rich, handsome, creative, independently minded former World War I fighter pilot, Darrin had an innate sense of style, proportion and balance that was demonstrated in an early aptitude for designing mechanical devices and automobiles. When only in his teens, he had invented an electric gearshift for John North Willys. He first went to France and fell in love with Paris during World War I as a flier and returned there in 1923 with Tom Hibbard to establish a custom coach-building business. Much of Darrin's work was for movie stars and the cream of European high society, and he came to know leading car makers of the day such as Andre Citroen, Louis Renault, the Panhard brothers and Ettore Bugatti.

By 1937, however, the European market for individual full-body custom coachwork was waning in the face of the deteriorating political situation with Germany. Darrin saw the writing on the wall and, with the assistance of his friend 20th Century–Fox executive Darryl F. Zanuck, he wisely moved back to Hollywood where he figured that film stars would be likely to invest in a more economic reworking of production cars in his unique style to render them individually distinctive. He opened his coachwork business on the Sunset Strip under the name of Darrin of Paris, putting together a strong work team that was soon busy on commissions for well-known actors Dick Powell, Chester Morris, and Clark.

Perhaps Clark saw Dick Powell driving around in his two-seater Packard Darrin roadster, or Chester Morris in the first Darrin Convertible Victoria, although there's another story that Clark's car was a birthday present from Carole Lombard (not a 1940 Darrin Convertible Victoria 180 as is sometimes claimed). In any case, Darrin's second Packard commission came from Clark, and it was this vehicle that really gained Darrin the recognition in Hollywood and with Packard that he so rightly deserved.

Clark's Darrin Convertible Victoria was based on the standard Packard Eight Business Coupe on a One Twenty chassis. Darrin liked working with Packard; he felt that their chassis was perfect and that the grille lines, from which he drew inspiration for his body designs, were truly classical. While Clark's Victoria is instantly identifiable as a unique Darrin design, enough of the original lines remain for the vehicle to still be unmistakably a Packard. Darrin stripped the Business Coupe's roof, doors, cowl, windshield and running boards, dropped the engine in its frame so he could lower the body, swept back the rear fenders for streamlining, curved and flared the rocker panels, strengthened the body with sill reinforcement, and narrowed and lengthened the hood by more than nine inches to reach back over the cowl to a cut-down windshield frame. He rebuilt the doors to incorporate sweeping curves along the top that from then on were such a characteristic signature they became known as the "Darrin Dip." He also tucked the dashboard and instrument panel under a roll of aircraft cockpit-style crash-padding. Eventually the team could turn out one of these Packard-Darrin conversions in two weeks.

However, while the Convertible Victoria undoubtedly looked spectacular, it wasn't without problems. The modified vehicle suffered from body flex because of the removal of the rigid roof, shake and rattle because of the wood-framed cowl, doors and rear seat, and front-end vibration because the lowered radiator had meant removal of the cradle. The door alignment could be so bad they would fly open on corners, and the top tended to leak badly in the rain. Later models had a cast aluminum cowl that made a difference, but it wasn't fitted to Clark's car. Apart from all that, just raising or lowering the fabric top involved the use of a complicated and time-consuming mechanism that took up most of the room in the trunk.

When completed, the Convertible Victoria probably cost Clark between $4,200 and $5,200, a lot of money in those days but quite reasonable compared to what he would have handed over for his Duesenberg JN convertible. Yet barely a month after Clark took delivery of this unique and expensive vehicle, he sold it. The legendary story quickly developed that the car's distinctiveness had led to legions of female fans following him and attempting to climb in whenever he drove out in it and stopped at the lights. However, Clark was a knowledgeable and discerning car owner and a capable mechanic; it's more likely that the vehicle's rather apparent flaws conflicted with the perfectionism of a man who could have any car he chose. Bear in mind it was Darrin, a great marketing man as well as designer, who promoted that story about Clark's female fans in a newspaper interview in late 1938. After all, customers were paying him a lot of money for a luxury car, not one that rattled, flexed and leaked like a Model T Ford and that could kill you if you fell out because a door opened without warning.

Many years later, Clark's Darrin Convertible Victoria was purchased by Ernest Sulek from a military officer in Cedar Rapids, Iowa, where it was discovered in 1962 by Sam Broadhead and his brother-in-law after having survived at least two floods. They purchased it and began restoration, during which they found beneath one of the seats a fishing license in the name of George Bruce. After some research, they discovered that it was the stage name of Andrew Bruce, a bit player who had been a friend of Clark's and to whom he had evidently sold the vehicle. Darrin could confirm that the car was the one he had worked on for Clark, because it had been the only Convertible Victoria on which he had stretched the hood to within half an inch of the door opening. In 1982, the car was acquired from the Broadheads by Ted Leonard, who had it repainted black and reupholstered with red leather, believing that this was the original color scheme. He kept it as part of his extensive collection for a quarter century. In June of 2009, it was sold to another private collector for $282,000.

In 1940, deafened by the clamor of dealers, Packard finally added the Darrin Convertible Victoria to the company's extensive offering of body styles, but they had their doubts about reduced body strength as a result of Darrin's conversions and didn't make any more after 1942. By then, Darrin had gone off to train pilots and be friends with Howard Hughes, and he never returned to Packard. He later designed for Kaiser-Frazer and contributed to the Jeep Wagoneer. One of his last projects was a Darrin version of the Rolls-Royce Silver Shadow.

Only 12 Convertible Victorias were built in California on the One Twenty chassis by Darrin; some of them were purchased by other stars such as Errol Flynn, Tyrone Power, Al Jolson, Rosalind Russell, Constance Bennett and drummer Gene Krupa. But, this would be Clark's last Packard. Like Darrin, he moved on. (I'm indebted to Bonhams & Butterfields Autions for information about Clark's Convertible Victoria.)

114 Clark must have lovingly polished a number of these Packard ornaments. The one on the '38 Convertible Victoria looks very much like a double-crested cormorant, used in several versions as the Packard mascot between 1932 until 1957, but Packard didn't actually call it a cormorant until 1939. It was originally known as a pelican, although this bird clearly lacks the bulkier body and the underbill pouch, because a pelican surmounts the Packard family's coat of arms, which appeared on some of the earlier models. The bird is a heraldic symbol of sacrifice, wounding her own breast so her young can feed on her blood. When the Ninth Series cars were to be introduced in 1932, Packard announced a competition for a new radiator emblem, but could not agree with any of the entries and so the design department produced their version of the pelican. Owners protested when the marketing department changed the name of the emblem because "cormorant" sounded more dig-

114 A close-up of the 1938 Packard Convertible Victoria's hood ornament (copyright © 2009 Bonhams & Butterfields Autioneers Corp. All rights reserved).

115 Clark looking very much the owner of Percy Morgan's unique Jensen-Ford in 1936 (courtesy the Gable Archive).

nified, but Packard didn't officially revert to "pelican" until 1951.

Packard used some other hood emblems, too, such as the Goddess of Speed and Adonis, sometimes known as Sliding Boy.

115–117 Like the SSJ Duesenberg roadster, this was a car that never actually belonged to Clark. When given the opportunity to own one of only three Jensen-Fords ever built for American importation, Clark declined because he didn't like the color.

The Jensen-Ford car in these photos was the joint product of some American creative business thinking and fine British engineering. Richard and Alan Jensen had begun designing and building car bodies while apprentices in the Birmingham, England, motor industry, and by 1930 they were doing so well working for others that they decided to start their own company. The following

116 Clark sitting in the Jensen-Ford that Morgan refused to sell him (courtesy the Gable Archive).

117   A current photograph of Percy Morgan's Jensen-Ford, now fully restored and part of the collection housed at 3 Dog Garage in Pennsylvania (with permission William Andresen).

year they went into partnership with W. J. Smith & Co., eventually assuming control after Smith's death and renaming the business Jensen Motors in 1936. On a visit to England the previous year, Edsel Ford had given the brothers permission to use Ford's new 3.6-liter V-8 engine and it was soon being incorporated into Jensen's well-reviewed four-seater tourer built on a Ford chassis, known as the "White Lady."

Some of those glowing write-ups were read that year in America by Percy Morgan, a Californian businessman, pioneer pilot, car enthusiast and friend and business associate of famous car body designer and builder "Dutch" Darrin. Morgan liked the Jensen style and wrote to the brothers about becoming a Hollywood agent for their cars. However, to avoid stiff English import duty, he proposed shipping his own Ford chassis to Jensen, who would then do the coachwork and ship the completed vehicle back to America. It sounded like a fairly simple idea until he ran into problems purchasing the chassis. Because Morgan was a private individual, not the owner of a car business, he discovered that Ford wouldn't sell him just a chassis. He would have to purchase it through a dealer after promising Ford the chassis wouldn't be used in building a race car.

So Morgan had to go to dealer Ham Nerney, of Nerney Ford in Los Angeles, and order the chassis to be shipped by the New Jersey factory to Jensen in England. All that took time, and so the completed vehicles did not arrive on the docks in Los Angeles until late 1936. Morgan initially ordered two cars: a black one with pigskin upholstery for himself as a personal car and demonstrator, and a silver vehicle with red leather upholstery for Clark Gable. Somehow, Morgan had managed to persuade the notoriously tight-fisted Clark to hand over a $1,000 deposit for a car he'd never even seen, yet had evidently omitted to ask Clark about his color preferences. Silver was never one of Clark's favorite colors.

The four-seat body was paneled in aluminum over a wood frame; the hood was lengthened; new shock absorbers could be adjusted from inside the cockpit by the driver; the steering column was raked; fully adjustable bucket seats were installed; and dual exhausts fitted. The front and rear fenders were re-shaped to follow the contour of new steel running boards, and flush-with-body electric turn indicators and high-powered Lucas head lamps were added.

When the cars arrived at the Wilmington docks, Morgan and Clark went down in one of the Nerney Ford trucks to pick them up. Clark had typically brought along some beer for the longshoremen and everyone pitched in to get them unloaded. Then the covers came off and Clark saw his new silver Jensen-Ford in the California sunlight for the first time. Immediately deciding he didn't like it, Clark asked Morgan whether he could have the black one instead, but Morgan had no desire to hand over his own precious, hand-built, personal car into which he had sunk so much of his time and money. Instead, he diplomatically suggested that Clark drive the silver one around for a while just to see how it felt. Ever gracious in defeat, and just to show they were still friends, Clark agreed and even happily posed with Morgan's car for the publicity shots you can see here. For a few days, he was occasionally seen around the streets of Beverly Hills in the silver Jensen-Ford, but then he returned it to the Nerney Ford dealership and used his deposit refund to buy a JN Duesenberg. That, by all accounts, is where his relationship with the Jensen-Ford ended.

Morgan's plans of being an importing agent pretty much ended there as well. He'd added his figures and realized this was not likely to be a profitable venture. Not only would the chassis have to travel from the U.S. to England and back again, but by the time the finished car was delivered to him in California it would cost $2300, including $1297 just for the Jensen body, and his selling price was already set at $2900! He did sell a third Jensen-Ford to Ted Wilcox from Portland, Oregon, but once again was dogged by problems when a shipping strike in England held up delivery. The resourceful Morgan had Gable's silver car painted black and sold that one to Wilcox instead.

Some 23 years later Morgan sold "Old Betsy," his black Jensen-Ford, to actor Robert Bray, who is now probably best remembered for playing forest ranger Corey Stuart in the *Lassie* television series. With plans in mind for building a hot rod, Bray dismantled it and stored it in a basement where it was eventually discovered and purchased by Warren Wyman, a wealthy building contractor and Ford car restoration enthusiast; years earlier while working as a gas station attendant he had seen Clark driving his Jensen-Ford around Beverly Hills. He went to work on a remarkable restoration in his workshop at Rancho Santa Fe, near San Diego, with the help of Morgan's photos and several trips to England to locate parts.

At about the same time, *Ford-Life* magazine co-publisher Gordon Chamberlin located the (originally silver) Jensen-Ford in the backyard of a Long Beach car collector, where it had been standing for years exposed to weather and falling into ruin. He restored and later sold that car, and it now belongs to a collector in North Carolina. When the third Jensen-Ford finally arrived, it was owned for some time by comic actor Mischa Auer. It may then have been owned by a film studio for use in movies and was eventually garaged in Sylmar, California. Recently sold, that car is also currently being restored. These are the only three Jensen-Fords of this type known to have been imported into the United States.

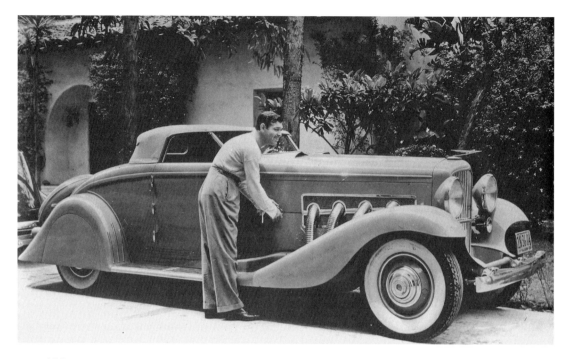

118   Clark lovingly closes the hood of his 1935 Duesenberg JN (SWB) Convertible Coupe with body by Bohman and Schwartz (courtesy Auburn Cord Duesenberg Museum Photo Collection).

Back in the U.K. perhaps 30 of the Jensen sports tourer bodies were matched to Ford chassis and engines during the mid-thirties. By 1936, they were superseded by the S-type Jensen. After 1938, about 12 H-Types were built with Nash straight-eight OHC engines, plus one fitted with a Lincoln V-12 engine that was imported into America but is now back in the U.K. being restored. After World War II, perhaps their most famous car would be the steel-bodied, Italian-designed Jensen Interceptor with its distinctive wrap-around rear glass window, built from 1966 to 1976. The earlier versions had 383-cubic inch Chrysler engines but the later Interceptor FF models, claimed to be the first production cars with all-wheel drive and anti-lock brakes, moved to 440-cubic inch engines.

In June 2008, Percy Morgan's still-immaculate black Jensen-Ford was sold at auction for $203,500. After Wyman passed away, it had become part of the collection of Robert Gottlieb, known for his "Classic Comments" column in *Motor Trend*. It has now been restored to Concours standard and, still fitted with its original V-8 engine and currently upholstered in cream leather with a tan soft top, is now part of the 3 Dog Garage collection in Pennsylvania.

118–119   This is the Duesenberg (Chassis #2585) that Clark owned, as opposed to the roadster that he had on loan. It was reputed to be a gift to Clark from his wife Carole and to be her favorite of all Clark's vehicles.

Popularly known then as "America's Mightiest Motor Car," Duesenbergs were built by the Auburn-Cord-Duesenberg Company in Auburn, Indiana, that had been established by financier Errett Lobban Cord and a pair of automobile engineer brothers, Fred and August Duesenberg. The Duesenberg brothers were skilled German immigrant racing bicycle builders and mechanics who began manufacturing cars in 1906 for Frank Maytag, of later washing machine fame. In 1913 they established the Duesenberg Automobile Company in St. Paul, Minneapolis and by 1917 they had built a larger plant in New Jersey to manufacture aircraft and tractor engines.

Finely tuned automobile engines were always their great love, though. In 1914, Eddie Rickenbacker drove a Duesenberg in the Indy 500, and Duesenbergs went on to win that race in 1924, 1925 and 1927. In 1919, a 16-cylinder Duesenberg set a land speed record of 158 mph at Daytona Beach, and in 1921 Jimmy Murphy drove a Duesenberg to become the first American to win a European Grand Prix in an American-built car, a record that held until 1960. In July 1921, the Duesenbergs moved to Indianapolis and began producing the Duesenberg Model A, the first American production passenger car with all-wheel hydraulic brakes, but they couldn't achieve successful commercial body designs and the business began to seriously struggle for survival.

Enter Errett Lobban Cord, a wealthy and renowned entrepreneur who'd twice been featured on the cover of *Time*. Cord wanted to create the finest motorcar in America and, already owner of the successful Cord Automobile Corporation which included the Auburn, proceeded to buy up Duesenberg in 1926. With the assistance of Fred Duesenberg in development, the Model J was introduced at the 1928 New York Automobile Salon. With a price tag of $8,500 for the chassis alone (the cost doubled with the addition of a custom-built body), it was no car for the common man but the rich and famous quickly lined up to buy them. Cord's timing could have been better. The following year the stock market crashed and the Depression was upon them all. The company struggled on for a few more years, but eventually could not survive the change in living brought on by a reduced economy.

119 This photograph of Clark's fully restored JN Duesenberg Convertible was taken by Tom Knight at the 2008 Amelia Island Concours in Florida (with permission Tom Knight).

While it lasted, though, the Duesenberg J and the later JN and SJ models were magnificent examples of a combination of design and engineering function. Their standard engine was a race-inspired vision of polished aluminum: a 265-horsepower, 32-valve, 420-cubic inch straight-eight built by Lycoming, known for its aircraft engines. The Model J's successor, the 320-horsepower supercharged SJ introduced in 1932, reached speeds of up to 140 mph. Fitted into J. Herbert Newport's streamlined body that became known as the Mormon Meteor, one of these engines was rebuilt to produce 400 horsepower at 5000 rpm and averaged 135.5 mph over 24 hours in 1935 on the Bonneville Salt Flats. The following year, a massive 1570-cubic inch Curtiss Conqueror V-12 was installed in the same car that, driven by Ab Jankins, had by the end of 1936 taken the 12-hour and 24-hour land speed records to 153.8 and 148.6 mph respectively, effectively making it the fastest vehicle on wheels in the world at that time. No wonder a Duesenberg marketing slogan was that the only car that could pass a Duesenberg was another Duesenberg — but only with the first driver's consent.

Between 1929 and 1937, Auburn Cord Duesenberg produced 481 Model J Duesenbergs of which some 378, including all but two of the custom-built speedsters, are known to still exist. Considering their age, that's a fitting tribute to the standard of craftsmanship in their construction. Many of these were re-bodied or had custom bodies especially made by hand for a particular chassis, and some of those bodies were then re-worked some years later for new owners, so it can appear that many more Duesenbergs were produced than was actually the case. Their owners were more often than not the *crème de la crème* of society, including candy magnates Phillip K. Wrigley and Ethel V. Mars, pharmaceutical magnate Josiah K. Lilly, razor blade industrialist Col. Jacob Schick, and any number of movie industry people. Bear in mind that it was not unusual for a completed top-of-the-line Duesenberg to cost $20,000 in an era when families waited in bread lines, and an average doctor's salary was less than $3,000 a year. A new Ford Model A roadster, by comparison, was about $450 in 1929, while a new Auburn family sedan could be bought for $1,000.

All JNs were sold with coachwork by Rollston. Clark had the firm of Bohman and Schwartz in Pasadena restyle his, including features such as flared front and rear fenders with hoods at the rear, double rear-mounted spares with solid covers and twin cowl vents. They also lowered and raked the windshield, and brought the hood all the way beyond the firewall to the windshield. Its 420-cubic inch engine was the most powerful you could buy unmodified on a dealership floor, enabling the two-and-a-half ton JN to hurtle down the highway at over 115 mph.

Clark owned this vehicle up until his wife Carole died, whereupon it was left in Canada with instructions that it never be seen again in California while he was still alive. In 1984 it was purchased from Parvis of England, who had never taken it out of the U.S., by the Blackhawk Collection. Now owned by Emily and Sam Mann, this immaculate ivory-cream JN has won a number of awards including the Best of Show at the 2008 Amelia Island Concours d'Elegance in Florida, and the Meadow Brook Hall Memorial Award at the 2008 Meadow Brook Concours d'Elegance.

120   Although Clark only drove it for a short time on loan, this Duesenberg Roadster (J-567, Chassis # 2595) is probably the most famous car associated with him. Only two of these Roadsters were ever built, and Gary Cooper was the only person who ever actually owned one (J-563, Chassis #2594) at the time. He'd had an earlier Duesenberg, a Derham Tourster or dual-cowl phaeton (J-431) with a roll-down rear windshield designed by Gordon Buehrig, the completed pale green and yellow version of which was sitting in the showroom when

120   A recent photograph of the 1935 Duesenberg SSJ (XSWB) Roadster with body by Central-Lagrande, driven on loan by Clark (courtesy Auburn Cord Duesenberg Museum Photo Collection).

Cooper saw it and bought it on the spot. Apparently Cooper brought the Tourster into the factory showroom one day for some minor work when he spotted the completed SSJ there and promptly traded the Tourster plus $5,000 for it, and then had the originally buff-colored Roadster painted two shades of grey.

For some reason, a pair of short-wheelbase roadster bodies had originally been supplied by the Central Manufacturing Company to LaGrande, Duesenberg's in-house coachbuilding department formed to sell the creations of their designer Gordon Buehrig. Central, based in Connersville, Indiana, was one of three body suppliers to Duesenberg and a subsidiary of E.L. Cord's business empire. The roadsters were eventually completed to a design by J. Herbert Newport, Jr. (1907–1991), who had become chief designer for Duesenberg in 1933 after Buehrig had left to work for Auburn. Newport had previously worked for Studebaker, Dietrich and Brunn as well as with Derham, and he became the man who really created the "look" of the Duesenberg. The two hand-built roadsters had the same supercharged eight-cylinder 400-horsepower engine as the SJ, making them capable of 100 mph in second and a top speed of 150 mph. Those engines were said to be the most powerful ever installed in a J model intended for street use. The Roadster pair eventually acquired the designation SSJ, although it was never officially used by Duesenberg.

Clark was allowed to have his Roadster on loan from the Los Angeles Duesenberg distributor for two months, almost certainly for the publicity value. Naturally, to a man like Clark who fully appreciated a finely crafted fast car, this roadster must have seemed like a dream come true, but evidently either he couldn't afford it or maybe Carole thought one "Duesy" in the family was enough because, although he eventually stretched out the loan to six months, he seems to have made no real effort to purchase it. Even for Gable, though, there was a limit to the dealer's patience and it had to be returned, no doubt reluctantly. It was refurbished and sold shortly thereafter to renowned jazz violinist George E. Stoll, who had joined the MGM music department in 1937 and was an Oscar-winning composer, musical director and conductor. His work can be heard in more than 90 films, including *Babes in Arms*, *Anchors Aweigh*, *The Student Prince*, *Viva Las Vegas* and *Made in Heaven*. Maybe he drove it to the studio regularly, just to show people there that he had the car Gable couldn't buy.

During the 1950s, at which time it was apparently a buff color, the Roadster was purchased from Stoll for $2,500 by D. Cameron Peck of Chicago who already owned Cooper's car. Until recently, the now red and silver SSJ had been owned for 45 years by Al Ferrara of Cleveland, Ohio, who also had a collection of Pierce Arrow cars. The roadsters were last seen together as a pair at the 2003 Meadow Brook Concours d'Elegance held on the grounds of Meadow Brook Hall at Oakland University in Rochester, Michigan.

When someone says, "Isn't that (object of choice) a real *doozy*," that word originally meant a "Duesy"—the Duesenberg.

121–122   Being an outdoors man who usually needed to carry camping and fishing and hunting gear when he drove off for some relaxation, Clark eventually saw the value of owning a "Woody" station wagon. In fact, so taken was he with the style that he owned more than one.

Station wagons were just coming into their own in the late thirties. Originally, they were just that: a horse-drawn wagon and eventually a modified vehicle that hauled people and luggage to and from a railroad station. They were also sometimes referred to as "depot hacks," a hack being a taxicab. In England, where they were often used for hunting, they were known as "shooting

brakes" or "estate wagons." The first "woodies" were custom-built vehicles with wood-framed rear sections paneled in wood for lightness, often built on a truck or heavy-duty vehicle chassis.

Ford was one of the first "woody" manufacturers. For the sake of reliability and consistency, Henry Ford began to acquire his own supplies of raw materials early in the history of the company, especially wood. The Upper Peninsula of Michigan attracted his attention for its largely untapped supplies of birch, maple and elm, hardwood timbers extensively used in cars of the twenties and thirties for frames, floors, trim, and wheels. A Model T, for example, could consume 250 board feet. By 1920, Ford owned over 400,000 acres of Upper Peninsula forest around the area of Iron Mountain, where the company built sawmills, a chemical treatment plant, drying kilns, show-case lumber camps, a hydro-electric plant and even the entire village of Kingsford, as well as facilities in three other counties.

121   **Clark driving one of his Woody Wagons (courtesy the Gable Archive).**

122   With one foot on the running board, Clark happily poses with his 1937 Ford Woody Wagon (courtesy the Gable Archive).

Ford offered an optional wooden body on a Model T frame as early as 1921. In the beginning, coach building firms such as Murray Body Company in Detroit took delivery of a complete chassis and then added the wooden bodywork parts that were shipped to them from Iron Mountain before returning the vehicle to the maker for final assembly. Murray Body and Mengle Products in Louisville, Kentucky, together supplied Ford with 9000 finished bodies a day until 1937 when they went to all-steel. After that, the Iron Mountain facilities produced Woody bodies complete and ready for the final touches until about 1951.

The 1937 Ford in the photograph was Clark's first Woody wagon, one of a total of 9304 produced that year at an average price of around $756. Although the exact number of unmodified survivors is unknown, fully restored examples of this wagon are rare today and consequently costly. One was sold by Christie's in 2007 for $159,500, another was sold by RM Auctions for $195,000 in 2008.

123–125   By 1939, Woodies were being used not just privately but as service vehicles for country clubs, hotels, country merchants, estates, and even for schools. They could carry up to eight people or the back seats could be removed to haul even more goods or luggage. Many a Hollywood star by now considered them a status symbol and Clark was no exception, so that year he picked up his second Woody.

This lovingly maintained version of a 1939 Ford Woody housed at the Mt. Dora Museum of Speed in Florida was fully restored frame-off through Early Ford V-8 Sales in Balston Spa, New York, in 2003. It was one of only 2,203 Standard model Woodies made that year with glass windows; others had side curtains. The bodies were still being made by Murray Corporation,

123 A magnificently restored 1939 Ford Woody, now part of the classic Dreamcars Collection at the Mt. Dora Museum of Speed in Florida (courtesy Classic Dreamcars & Mt. Dora Museum of Speed, Florida).

and they could be outfitted with such niceties as dome lights, leather seats, super "deep dish" beveled lens fog-lamps (or road-lamps), a ventilating fan, heavy duty clutch, roof-top removable luggage carrier, and whitewall tires. Extra options included a "banjo-style" steering wheel, Columbia overdrive, radio, heater, and glove box or visor-mounted clock. The spare tire was mounted inside on the back of the driver's seat, instead of near the tailgate. This Model 79 vehicle has an 85hp flathead V-8 with three-speed floor-mounted shift, Ford's first Lockheed Aircraft-designed hydraulic brakes, and solid maple body.

However, the great Woody era was yet to come. With steel in short supply during the war years, and then immediately after, partial wooden vehicle bodies were as necessary an economic measure as they were a style feature. Ford alone built some 160,000, along with lesser productions from such makers as Plymouth, Chevrolet, Pontiac, Mercury and Packard. Clark also owned a 1940 Buick Woody Wagon, along with a legendary one-off custom built 1939 Dodge Woody. Ford finally ended production of real Woodies in 1953, but continued with the side-paneled woody "look" on its 1960s Country Squire Station Wagons (Clark had one).

The 1939 Woody in the photograph above carries on the luggage rack a set of genuine vintage leather luggage complete with gun scabbard, antique fishing rod, reel and creel, wood shaft gold clubs and matching bags, and steamer trunk. I like to think it looks very much as if

it was parked outside the ranch house at Encino, just waiting for Clark and Carole to step in and head off for La Grulla or to hunt with the Fleischmans at Bakersfield.

124 This is what Clark would have seen inside the cab of his 1939 Ford Woody Wagon (courtesy Classic Dreamcars & Mt. Dora Museum of Speed, Florida).

126 The story of Clark's Jaguar cars has grown larger with the passing of time, much like the reputation of the vehicles themselves. Gable ownership has been claimed for a number of Jaguars over the years, particularly amongst the small group of 240 1949 alloy-bodied XK 120s that were built. So far, however, known documentation only supports Clark's

125 Perhaps Clark and Carole might have carried some of these things in the back of their Woody (courtesy Classic Dreamcars & Mt. Dora Museum of Speed, Florida).

126 At Roger Barlow's International Motors on Wilshire Boulevard, Clark is behind the wheel of his 3.5-liter Mark IV Jaguar drophead coupe in conversation with Roger Barlow (courtesy www.jaguarmagazine.com).

ownership of a Mark IV and a Mark V drophead coupe and two XK120s. He was loaned a third XK120 by the then-owner of the Indianapolis Raceway. So there, as they say, hangs a tale and certainly in the case of Clark and his Jaguars there is a number of them.

The Jaguar car company began in 1922 as Swallow Sidecars, founded by William (later Sir William) Lyons and William Walmsley. From 1927 they branched out into motor vehicle coach building for such companies as Austin and did so well that 12 months later the business moved to larger premises in Coventry. In the early thirties, the name was changed to SS Cars Ltd and from 1936 to 1940 they produced the SS100 sports car. Initially built in a 2.5-liter version, it was also offered with the larger 3.5- liter engine after 1938 that easily enabled the car to reach speeds of 100 mph. After World War II the company was renamed Jaguar, largely because of the unwelcome connotations of the SS letters. During the war years, they had ceased building cars but then in the mid-forties they re-started production of what were essentially post-war versions of their pre-war models, offering a four-cylinder 1.5-liter saloon and six-cylinder 2.5-liter and 3.5-liter saloons and drop-head coupes. The latter could achieve 100 mph with ease and so was just the kind of car to interest Clark, who was in the market for a new sports car when he emerged from military service.

Clark started dropping by Roger Barlow's International Motors on Wilshire Boulevard in Beverly Hills during 1946. Barlow was the agent for a number of European sports car marques such as MG, Riley, Jaguar and Mercedes-Benz, and Clark enjoyed hanging around, looking over the exotic cars, talking shop and doing some wishing. Eventually he left the number of his personal assistant, Jean Garceau, and asked Barlow to contact her when something interesting came in. As it turned out, Clark was away on location when Barlow's first shipment of new Mark IV Jaguars arrived: five SS100 sedans and two Mark IV drop-head coupes. By the

127   Seated proudly in his new 1949 XK120, Clark chats with the man who created it, William Lyons, who would be knighted in 1956 (courtesy www.jaguarmagazine.com).

128   At home, Clark stands alongside his new 1949 XK120, registered in California as 56A-2443 (courtesy Carole Sampeck/Carole Lombard Archive).

129   Clark inspects what is under the hood of his new car (courtesy www.jaguarmagazine.com).

time Clark showed up at the showroom, only one metallic silver drophead coupe remained unsold and even that one was in the process of being bought by publishing executive Hastings Harcourt. When Clark said he wanted to drive it home immediately, Barlow was faced with a dilemma that he solved in a typically sporting manner: They tossed a coin for it. Clark called heads and won. A week later, when Clark returned to have a small dent repaired, he mentioned that he didn't particularly like the car's color, so the two men mixed and matched some paint until he and Barlow came up with a shade of dark gray that would become known as "Gable Gray." The Mark IV was duly re-sprayed, and Clark's other Jaguars would each be painted that color in turn.

127–129   Both the Mark V and the XK120 were unveiled in London at the Earls Court Automobile Show in 1948. The Mark V was a streamlined version of the Mark IV, still offered with 2.5 and 3.5 motors with four-door saloon or drophead coupe bodies. Clark bought one and drove it for awhile, but he was really just waiting for the first XK120 sports car to arrive.

The fluid body curves of the XK120 were said to have been personally designed by William Lyons, now general manager of Jaguar Cars Ltd. The 3.4-liter, six-cylinder DOHC engine could propel the car to over 120 mph, hence the model number. Jaguar thought they could probably sell 250 of the new cars, the total of the planned initial production run for the two-seater roadster, but delays in producing the required steel body molds prompted the building of 240

bodies with panels that were hand-cut and beaten from sheets of aluminum alloy. Because these vehicles were hand-crafted, no two were exactly alike; the panels from one car wouldn't fit the other. This early alloy-bodied version quickly proved successful in sports car events. During a motorway speed test in Belgium, Clark's second XK120 (Chassis #660986 that would be registered as MDU 524) clocked 172.4 mph making it at the time the fastest series production car in the world.

In late 1949, after he had completed work in Hollywood on *Any Number Can Play*, Clark was finally able to take delivery of his new aluminum-bodied XK120 that had been shipped to Los Angeles. Roger Barlow wrote an article that appeared in the February 27, 1989, issue of *Autoweek* in which he claims that Clark specifically requested that the first XK120 to arrive in California be reserved for him. However, Barlow writes, when the first of the new models was unloaded it was immediately apparent that this one was intended for display purposes only because it was minus a crankshaft. Nevertheless, as promised,

130   "Honestly, honey, I can put this all back together again." This is the XK120, chassis #670003, currently being restored in the U.K. (with permission JD Classics).

Clark still had the first ride. Barlow attached one end of a rope to the Jaguar, in which Clark sat behind the wheel, then the other end to a truck with which he hauled Clark and his car out into the L.A. streets. Once they reached an appropriate speed, the rope was released and Gable experienced his first "drive" including a four-wheel slide across rain-wet pavement as he maneuvered the car around a corner back into the dealership garage. Grinning from ear to ear, Clark rolled the car to a stop while onlookers, staff and mechanics cheered and applauded. A few days later, Clark took delivery of an XK120 he could actually drive home, registered in California as 56A-2443.

It is quite possible that the display vehicle could have been the cream car that some people recall Clark referring to as the car he was buying, because Jean Garceau clearly remembered that the XK-120 Clark brought home was gray with red upholstery and a number of photos of him with the car, including some with Sir William Lyons, seem to bear that out. On the other hand, Barlow was well aware of Clark's preference for gray and so his car could well have been given a quick color change from factory cream to "Gable Gray" before he drove it out the dealership door. Photos such as these confirm the link between Clark and 56A-2443 and this registration number has in turn been linked to Chassis #670003, the third left-hand-drive XK120 built by Jaguar and the first sold in the U.S.

Clark had been guaranteed by the dealer that his new car could reach speeds of 128 mph, and he would regularly test that figure out on the desert salt flats. Jean Garceau recalled that he reached 125 mph on one memorable occasion while she was sitting alongside him. Clark

131   Looking worried in case the paint has been scratched, Clark inspects his new Jaguar XK120, chassis #672282, registered MDU420, as it is being delivered to him in Cornwall in June 1952. (If you look very carefully, you can see a person holding a child in their arms reflected in the door, and the photographer is reflected on the front fender between the bumper and the headlight) (courtesy www.jaguarmagazine.com).

132   Photographed from the other side, Clark tries out the driving position in his new car. As you can see by all the bystanders, the delivery has generated some excitement (courtesy www.jaguarmagazine.com).

enjoyed the car so much that he penned a special feature article entitled "My Favorite Sports Car" in a 1950 issue of *Road and Track* magazine expressing his high opinion of it.

130 Until that link between registration number and chassis number is established by original documentation, #670003 remains at this time the most likely vehicle to be the 1949 Gable XK120.

According to the Classical Jaguar Association XK120 Register, Clark never actually sold this car. Instead, he presented it as a gift to William Caracciola, son of the great German Formula One racing driver of the 1930s, Rudolph Caracciola. Eventually, it became part of Wesley Clark's collection in Texas, and in 2008 it was purchased by Derek Hood and taken back to the U.K. where it is currently being restored by JD Classics.

133 Looking every inch a local, Clark pauses while driving along the coast in his new car, probably in Cornwall where he was working in *Never Let Me Go* (courtesy www.jaguarmagazine.com).

131–133 In late May 1952, while Clark was staying at the Dorchester in London preparing for his role in *Never Let Me Go*, he arranged through the Hornburg dealership in Los Angeles to buy a new XK120SE with wire wheels. Classified as a personal export delivery vehicle, registered in England as MDU420 and already painted gray, this vehicle was delivered from the factory in Coventry to Clark. By this time he was on location down in Cornwall, and this is where the above photos were taken to mark the occasion. After that, this car became a very well-traveled XK120 indeed.

When his work on the film was done, Clark had his new car flown across the Channel in late September to La Touquet in France. From there, he drove it into Switzerland and on through Italy to Rome, where he had the car stored while he flew to Kenya to star in *Mogambo*. When they were finished, his car was flown back to England to meet him. Then, Clark took it across the Channel again to Paris where he met up with his friends the Menascos and his girlfriend at the time, Suzanne Dadolle. Clark drove the car to Holland while he worked in *Betrayed*; then he finally brought it back to the U.S. when he returned to Encino in time for Christmas 1953. At that time, he had rear wheel spats with cut-outs for the wheel spinners fitted along with a louvered hood that would improve air circulation to better cool the engine.

By then, Clark may well have considered he'd spent enough time in a small cockpit and, besides, there were now quite a few miles on the odometer. In February 1954, he sold the Jaguar to the wealthy philanthropist and book collector Irving W. Robbins, Jr., for approxi-

134 Clark surveying some of the road well-traveled standing alongside his 1949 Ford Deluxe Club Coupe at the end of July 1950, while on his road trip from Los Angeles to Durango for location shooting of *Across the Wide Missouri* (courtesy John McElwee).

mately $4,000. Although the sale was finalized on February 16, the bill of sale from British Motor Car Distributors Ltd. that Clark signed, with Jean Garceau signing as witness, carries the later date of March 15 because the Department of Motor Vehicles mixed up the paperwork and a replacement document had to be made out. Robbins later wrote to Gable thanking him for helping to smooth out the problems with the sale and remarking on the wonderful care Gable had given the car.

In 1950, while Clark was working on the racing track scenes for the film *To Please a Lady* at the Indianapolis 500 track, he was loaned a green XK120 by the then-owner of the track. That car is currently on display at the IMS Museum. In an early scene of this movie, which would have been shot on the MGM lot, Clark walks into a workshop to look at a race car and gives an admiring glance at an XK120 sitting there with the hood up. It was reputedly his own car.

135 Perhaps the "gas jockey" is trying to figure out if this long-distance driver could really be Clark Gable during the *Across the Wide Missouri* road trip (courtesy John McElwee).

134–136 On July 28, 1950, Clark set out on a 1,000-mile road trip in his 1949 Ford Coupe from Los Angeles to Durango, Colorado, where William "Wild Bill" Wellman had assembled over 200 cast and crew and 22 truck-loads of equipment for the location shooting of *Across the Wide Missouri* in the San Juan Basin. Meanwhile, Clark's recent bride Lady Sylvia was traveling to Durango by train where she would meet him.

You would have to say that the car looks well-prepared, right down to the water-bags hanging at the front. Those were the days when the gas station attendant wore a uniform; he looks puzzled as he tries to add up how much Clark owes him on his fingers.

136 Clark makes sure that all is in order inside the Ford (courtesy John McElwee).

137   Perhaps the least likely of all the Gable cars, his Newport Blue 1954 Cadillac Coupe DeVille is photographed here outside the Gable birthplace museum in Cadiz, Ohio, where it is garaged (courtesy Clark Gable Birthplace Museum).

138   A front view of the Cadillac on display in the museum (courtesy the Gable Archive).

139   Clark showing off his 1956 Mercedes 300SC Cabriolet (courtesy Bruce Meyer).

This Ford Deluxe Club Coupe came with optional extras. Because it was Clark's Ford Deluxe, it would have been fitted with all of them such as that chrome grill guard and the large sun visor above the windshield. The large cylinder attached over the passenger-side window may have been an early air-cooler; he certainly would have needed one traveling down that way in summer. This new model was Ford's first post–World War II product line, and its

140–141 Side views of the restored Gable Mercedes Cabriolet, now owned by Bruce Meyer (courtesy Dennis Adler).

smooth streamlined curves became very popular. They were quickly nicknamed "shoebox" Fords because of their slab-sided bodies. Knowing Clark, this one was probably the 239-cubic inch, 100hp V-8 model and it was probably red.

137–138 More a car built for comfort than for speed, this personally customized Cadillac was ordered by Clark from Casa de Cadillac in Sherman Oaks, California, and he took delivery on July 15, 1954. It came with all the factory accessories including air conditioning (in only the second year it was available), a foot switch for the radio, power windows and driver's seat, power brakes and power steering. It also had a few personal touches ordered by Clark such as Eldorado trim, gold crests, ribbed quarter panel trim and specially designed hubcaps.

Clark drove the Caddy for a few years, but not very often, before selling it to a Mr. Schraff who in turn sold it to the Cars of the Stars Museum in Niagara Falls, Ontario, where it was displayed until the museum closed in 1979. Eventually it was purchased during the eighties for his classic car collection by Jim McCartney of Freeport, Ohio, near Clark's hometown of Cadiz, where it is now displayed at the Gable Birthplace and Museum. Maintained in drivable condition, it makes an occasional appearance in parades in the area. The odometer now has a little over 22,600 miles on it.

139–141 This tobacco-brown 300SC Cabriolet with cognac leather interior was said to have become Clark's favorite car, at least until he bought his Gullwing. It was elegant in a masculine kind of way while at the same time it was unpretentious. Purchased from Auto Stiegler, the Beverly Hills Mercedes-Benz dealership, this car was customized to order like many other Gable cars and most of his clothes, coming complete with hand-crafted chrome parts individually numbered for each vehicle and a trunk that held dual spare wheels, a roll of factory tools and custom-made fitted luggage. Clark was so proud of this car that when he and his wife Kay were offered the customary studio limousine for the 1956 premiere of the Warner Brothers film *Giant,* they declined and arrived in their Mercedes instead.

Throughout much of Europe, the World War II battlefield had extended right up to the front doors of the world's oldest and most established automakers, so there were precious few luxury automobiles available outside of America for the rest of that decade. However, by the early 1950s, Mercedes-Benz cars of unrivaled performance and style were once again being manufactured by Daimler-Benz AG, a company effectively created in 1926 with the formal merger of the two German car builders Benz & Cie and Daimler Motoren Gesellschaft. The new company had agreed that its factories would thereafter use the brand name of Mercedes-Benz on their automobiles, primarily designed and built by Wilhelm Maybach, a name that had originated when company director Emil Jellinek ordered a number of race cars to be built by Maybach with engines named after his daughter Mercedes.

The 300SC, introduced at the 1955 Paris Auto Show, was the sportier two-door model of the 300 series with a shorter wheelbase. Available as a coupe, cabriolet or roadster, it cost approximately $14,500 when new, over double the $6,800 price of a 1955 Gullwing 300SL and more than any American luxury car. The usual cost of a 1957 Cadillac Eldorado, for example, was a little over $6,600. Of the 200 Mercedes 300SC built between 1955 and 1958, only 49 were Cabriolets. Its 2996cc six-cylinder engine with Bosch mechanical fuel-injection, the first in a non-sports car, produces 175 horsepower and is capable of powering the cabriolet to speeds of over 110 mph. In short, the 300SC Cabriolet was the ideal combination of speed, luxury and style that typically defined a Gable car.

After Clark's death, Kay left the Cabriolet parked in the garage of their Encino home for over 20 years, finally selling it to collector Bruce Meyer in 1982 with only 32,000 miles on it. She also sold him the matching luggage and Clark's personally engraved St. Christopher medal on the dashboard.

Bruce Meyer, who has driven drag cars and dirt bikes, has been collecting cars for over 40 years now and his cars have won many awards at the Pebble Beach Concours d'Elegance alone. He is the former chairman of the Petersen Automotive Museum in Los Angeles, where one whole gallery is devoted to a rotating display of his collection that ranges through dozens of vehicles from cars of the twenties and thirties such as Duesenbergs and Pierce-Arrows through a 1940 Ford Coupe, a '56 Mercedes SL Gullwing, dragsters, hot rods, and Indy 500 racing cars to a Ferrari 275GTB4. A man with whom I'm sure Clark would have liked to pass the time talking about cars, Meyer also considers that the most important thing to do is drive them; they never sit idle in the garage.

The 300SC Cabriolet marked the passing of an era; Mercedes-Benz would never produce their like again.

142–145   Clark started thinking about purchasing this Mercedes 300SL Gullwing as soon as he saw it displayed at Mercedes-Benz of Hollywood in March 1955. With a mechanic's appreciation for the precision engineering that went into the car, Clark would take it for test runs, lift the hood and lovingly examine the motor, then come home and fret. They already had the Cabriolet, and Clark would typically worry that wanting another Mercedes was just being extravagant. Finally, Kathleen told him to go buy it; after all, he'd worked hard and he'd earned it. She went with him and they both signed the registration papers. However,

142   Clark's 1955 Mercedes 300 SL Gullwing Coupe, photographed in 2010 by Ann Sherman (courtesy www.annshermanphoto.com).

143 A front view of the Gullwing, showing the unique door configuration when open that gave this model its name (courtesy www.annshermanphoto.com).

144 The Gullwing's interior showing the dashboard (courtesy www.annshermanphoto.com).

145   The Gullwing's rear interior showing Clark's custom-fitted red leather luggage (courtesy www.annshermanphoto.com).

that didn't mean she got to drive it; Clark once let her and the car fight it out for a block and then declared she didn't have the touch.

This Gullwing would be his last favorite car; he adored it, often saying that climbing in and out of the low-slung car kept him young. When it came time to leave home for Reno to work on *The Misfits*, he insisted on driving the Gullwing so he could let it out on some of the long straight sections of highway. While he was down there, he and cinematographer Doc Kaminsky, who was making a documentary of the *Misfits* shoot in Nevada and was driving a new Austin-Healey, once raced each other across the desert over the Geiger Grade.

The Gullwing design came about through the campaigning of American Mercedes importer Max Hoffman, who finally persuaded Mercedes to build a road version of their 1952 300SL that had won at Le Mans. Consequently, they produced two models: the 300SL (W 198) and the smaller open-top 190 SL (W 121). Only 1400 of the 300SL series were produced between 1954 and 1957, costing some $7,500 in the U.S. They had the world's first direct-injection, three-liter six-cylinder gas engine not in a race car; able to reach 65 mph in ten seconds, these cars could do more than 100 mph with ease. The center of gravity is almost exactly in the middle of the car, making for incredible cornering at high speed. The entire car only weighs 2850 pounds complete with spare wheel, tools and fuel.

The streamlined sheet steel and aluminum skin was stretched over a lightweight, welded tubular space-frame designed by Rudolph Uhlenhaut. Because the frame rose much further up the sides of the vehicle than in a typical car design, it blocked the usual door spaces.

146 Clark dressed in the least likely outfit to ride a 1941 Harley-Davidson "Knucklehead" twin (courtesy Clark Gable Birthplace Museum, Ohio).

The occupants have to climb over the high sill and into the cockpit, and side-hinged doors would not allow enough room to do this. So, the concept of "gull-wing" doors that were hinged at the top was really born out of necessity rather than being just a quirky design feature.

After Clark's death, his Mercedes 300SL was sold to Harry Haenigsen, creator of the "Penny" comic strip, who later sold it to theme park entrepreneur Charles R. Wood. Wood kept it for 30 years until in 2003, at age 89, he sold it to Tom Davies in Oklahoma City.

Clark replaced the standard steel wheels with Rudge racing wheels and knock-off hubs and he may have had the standard white rim steering wheel, which could be folded down for driver access, replaced with the current wood and chrome Nardi wheel. Still equipped with Clark's custom-fitted leather luggage, it's been maintained just as if Clark was going to walk up any day, climb in and drive off to Nevada.

146–147 An enduring love of motorcycles led Clark to own a number of bikes. Most of his Harley-Davidsons were bought from West Coast distributor Rich Budelier, such as this 1942 61-cubic inch "Knucklehead" Twin that could do 100 mph. In 1979, Joe Hasset, who was then a roofer living in Ashtabula, Ohio, purchased an old Harley-Davidson motorcycle for $3000 at an auction in Tampa, Florida, because he was intrigued by the unusual 61-cubic inch engine. Covered in dust and dirt, the machine had been stored for 36 years. Knowing nothing about the Harley at the time, Hasset heard some rumors about a previous owner and

147   Clark's 1941 Harley-Davidson motorbike on display in the Gable birthplace museum (courtesy the Gable Archive).

after some research on the engine number he was able to confirm that he was now the proud owner of Clark's 1942 Knucklehead.

Apparently Clark had ridden it while he was training at OCS in Florida and had put it in storage when he was shipped out; it still had only 26,000 miles on it. The Harley was in such good condition that Hasset didn't even have to do any work on the motor, just replacing the tires and the rotted seat. Once he cleaned off the dirt, it started right up. In the leather military-style saddlebags he found a brand-new set of original tools that had come with the bike. The white-painted gas tank was apparently a custom color done for Gable. In 2002 this Harley-Davidson, estimated to be worth probably $100,000 by then, was badly damaged in a head-on collision in which Hasset was seriously injured.

Clark's first motorcycle may well have been a 1934 Harley-Davidson "45," named after its cubic inch capacity. The Harley-Davidson RL Model D flat-head had been introduced in 1929 as a competitor to Indian's successful 750cc side-valve v-twin. Soon all Harley's mainstream roadsters, regardless of capacity, would have flat-head engines. By 1934, when Clark purchased his RL, the 45's frame and front forks had been redesigned and engine improvements had been made. The high-compression RL had a strengthened frame, improved valve springs, larger flywheels and a new four-plate clutch, while demonstrating the powerful influence of art deco in their flamboyant fenders and striking paint schemes. Gable eventually sold his RL to David Fusiak of Garrison, New York. In November 2007, engine number 34RL2748 was

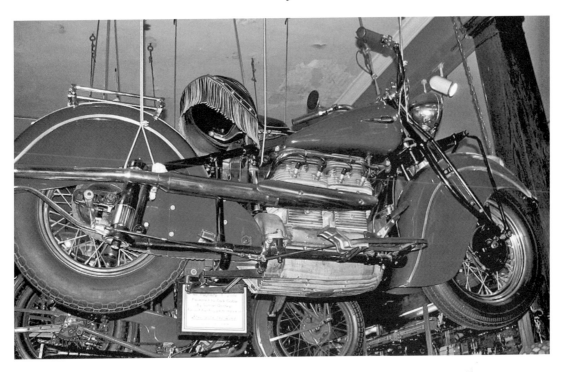

148 The sign (see below) says it all. Clark's 1941 four-cylinder Indian motorcycle hangs today from the ceiling of Capt. Eddie Rickenbacker's bar-restaurant in San Francisco (courtesy Bart Madson, www.motorcycle-usa.com).

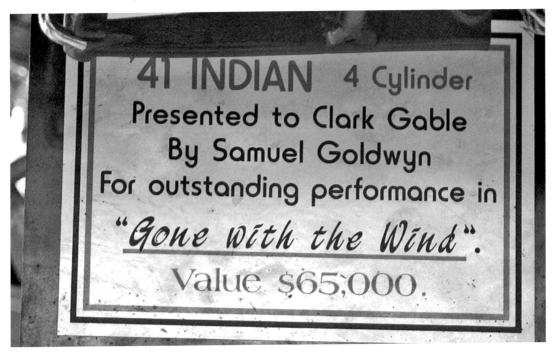

149 The sign beneath Clark's Indian motorcycle (courtesy Bart Madson, www.motorcycle-usa.com).

150 Squinting into the bright Los Angeles sun, Clark stands with his friend Ben Campanale, champion Harley Davidson rider and mechanic, outside the service department of Rich Budelier's Los Angeles Harley dealership in 1942 (courtesy www.theriderfiles.com).

sold to its fifth owner for $60,000. The red Harley-Davidson is now on display in the window of a certain well-known retail store in New York City.

148–149 The 1941 Indian currently hanging in Capt. Eddie Rickenbacker's Bar in San Francisco was given to Clark by Samuel Goldwyn for his work in *Gone with the Wind*. He also owned a Triumph Trophy and a Square Four Ariel that he rode while stationed at the Molesworth and Pole-brook air bases in England during World War II. Clark had little patience with out-of-date equipment, though, and preferred to trade in his bikes every year for the latest models, just as he did his cars. He was as meticulous with motorcycle maintenance as he was with his cars, too, putting in many hours tuning, tweaking and polishing.

150 At the age of 25, after beginning his racing career in his native New England, Ben Campanale had been the first rider to win the Daytona 200 two years in succession, 1938 and 1939. When this photo was taken in 1942, he was recovering from a bad multiple-rider accident at the Oakland track in which two riders had died. It had put him in a hospital for months, after which he had gone back to keeping his hand in as a mechanic while he was waiting to be strong enough to ride again.

In 1938 "Campy" had established his own dealership in Pomona, then known as Campy's Motorcycle Shop, which still exists today as Pomona Valley Harley-Davidson (PVHD). Clark always got a big kick out of having Campanale work on his bikes; he'd stop by regularly and continued to do so after the war until Ben sold the shop in 1948. Sometimes they'd have lunch together; Campy always remembered that Clark's favorite lunch dish was macaroni and cheese.

Clark was known to help some of the local bike racers out financially so they could make it to the next race. He'd look out for these guys by helping them get work as extras and in stunts on movie sets. Those racers really appreciated what Clark did, but he never wanted any

151 Three members of the "Morago Spit and Polish Club" all revved up with somewhere to go: (left to right) Clark, Ward Bond and Victor Fleming. Clark is still wearing his World War II leather flying jacket with its unit patch (courtesy Carole Sampeck/Carole Lombard Archive).

credit for it. He just did it because he liked the bravery of the riders. Ben said it seemed that Clark felt a kinship with them.

Ben, who passed away in April 2003, was inducted into the Motorcycle Hall of Fame in 1998, and he has been immortalized on the Daytona 200 monument in Florida.

151 During 1942, Clark became good friends with Al Menasco who also owned a motorcycle and they'd often ride out together at night through Ventura. Soon others joined them such as Bill Wellman and his wife, Ward Bond, Victor Fleming on his 995 Ariel Square Four, Howard Hawks, Andy Devine, Keenan Wynn, Tom Bamford and John Duncan. Wynn was friends with Bamford, a race car driver who owned a motorcycle shop across the street from Warners Studio, as well as Duncan who played Robin in the 1949 *Batman and Robin* serial; the trio were all Triumph Thunderbird riders who used to enjoy competing with the Harley riders in the group.

Ward Bond was also a great friend of John Wayne and director John Ford, for whom he worked in some two dozen films, but there are some intriguing similarities between him and Clark. They were very close to the same height and build, and the duration of their film careers was about the same number of years. Bond, however, appeared in many more movies within those years as well as on television, becoming famous in the last few years of his life in the series *Wagon Train*. Clark, on the other hand, always flatly refused to have anything to do with TV, except for a single appearance on *The Ed Sullivan Show*. During their contemporary careers, Clark and Bond appeared in just three movies together and, of those, Bond was only credited in *Gone with the Wind*. He passed away 11 days before Clark.

Victor Fleming and Clark were also good friends; Fleming directed or was involved in the direction of five Gable movies, most famously *Gone with the Wind*. They had much in common in terms of their characters, tastes and lifestyle. Like Clark, Fleming was tough, handsome and forthright and said just what was on his mind. He, too, was a mechanic and lover of fast cars who had actually been a race car and stunt driver at one time; this was how he had first become involved in movies. From stunt work he had turned to camerawork so successfully that he was soon directing; his first major movie was *The Virginian* (1929), which made a star of Gary Cooper. It was Fleming's work with Gable for *Red Dust* that had done wonders for Clark's career and established their friendship; Clark never forgot a person who had done him a good turn.

Various members of the group would frequently convene on Sundays in the driveway of Howard Hawks' home in Morago Drive before heading out on their motorcycles, often to Calabasas in the San Fernando Valley where the professional cyclists trained on a particular hill. The men would watch and occasionally have a try themselves. They liked to let their bikes out on long straight stretches of road where one of their favorite games was a form of tag at 90 miles an hour. However, competition among them was not usually over who had the fastest bike but who had the shiniest. Not for nothing were they known locally as the "Morago Spit and Polish Club." Hawks even had sweatshirts printed up.

Clark had a solid reputation for his excellent riding, for which he was respected widely in Hollywood even among the younger actors. Referring to the practice of wearing a steel sole that fitted over the bottom of the rider's boot so that you could drop your foot to the ground as you cornered at a sharp angle, James Dean once marveled admiringly that Gable was a real "hot shoe."

Social Life

152–153 At the time these pictures were taken, George Bernard Shaw was making a very uncharacteristic visit to MGM as part of his world tour, basically because Marion Davies was filming his play *Peg o' My Heart*. He and his wife stayed at San Simeon for a week, reputed to be the only time he actually slept on American soil. On their way to the studio for this lunch, their plane got caught in fog and was forced to land on Malibu Beach.

Probably remembered in present times because she was so memorably caricatured as the jigsaw-puzzling Susan Alexander, mistress of Citizen Kane in Orson Welles' classic film, Davies was in reality a talented and witty comedienne, brilliant mimic and excellent actor. With a movie career history that went back to 1917, she would most likely have been a successful star in her own right without William Randolph Hearst's rather heavy-handed assistance. Her early movies were released through Paramount, but in 1923 Hearst moved the Cosmopolitan production company that he had created for Davies to MGM, where she had a two-story, 14-room bungalow as her "dressing room."

In this MGM home-away-from-home, the Shaw dinner took place. Clark was there not just in recognition of his star status but also because he was a close friend of Davies, though it hadn't always been that way. Clark had been very unhappy about being requisitioned into Davies' 1932 movie *Polly of the Circus*, so much so that he went into hiding in Palm Springs and held out for a raise. Surprisingly, Davies actually supported him and persuaded Hearst to have Mayer draw up a new contract for Gable that would give him what he was asking. So, although *Polly* turned out to be pretty much the flop that Gable suspected it would be, he was a happier and richer man nonetheless and never forgot the favor Davies had done for him. They became lifelong friends and could often be seen during the early and mid-thirties strolling along Santa Monica's Ocean Walk and riding the roller coaster together. As it turned out, Davies would do Clark other favors that would affect his life, albeit unwittingly. Because she persuaded Mayer to trade Clark for Paramount's Bing Crosby in another picture, Clark would work with Carole Lombard for the first time while they appeared together in *No Man of Her Own*, and it was as a member of Davies' party that Clark attended the 1936 White Mayfair Ball where he and Lombard were first seen dancing together in public.

Charlie Chaplin was at the table because he had met Shaw the year previously at a luncheon at the Astors' home, Cliveden, while he was visiting England for the premiere of *City Lights*. To his surprise and trepidation, he then found himself seated next to Shaw for the performance itself, but they had parted affably.

147

152   Some of the diners at Marion Davies' dinner for George Bernard Shaw in 1933: Charlie Chaplin, George Bernard Shaw, Marion Davies, Louis B. Mayer, Clark Gable and George Hearst (courtesy the Gable Archive).

153   Clark with Marion Davies (courtesy the Gable Archive).

154 Clark alongside his Ford station wagon with the Barnard family's boxer dog, Guess, at their ranch in Ventura, California (courtesy Kinsey Barnard).

During his visit, Shaw seemed to think that insulting people was a demonstration of his wit. Before this photo was taken, John Barrymore had left the table in a rage when Shaw refused to autograph a page for his six-month-old son's album, saying he'd be too young to appreciate it. It was finally suggested the time might have come for Shaw to depart MGM after he informed Ann Harding, who had acted in his play *Androcles and the Lion* while Shaw was actually in the audience, that he didn't remember her and that if she had been in that play then it must have been an illegal, pirated version. As he stalked out, he declared that filmmaking didn't matter anyway because "it will never last. It's no good. It's phony." Marion may have scored a point in the end, though. Shaw was later heard to say she was by far the most attractive of the stars he had seen.

154–155 When Montana-based photographer Kinsey Barnard was a little girl, Clark and his wife Kathleen were frequent guests at her family's citrus and avocado ranch near what was once a small town known as Ventura, about 30 miles south of Santa Barbara and 60 miles north of Los Angles on the California coast. Her great grandfather, Austin Denny Barnard, had come to San Buena Ventura in the mid–1800s and her grandfather, Charles Ventura Barnard, was born there in 1869. In fact the original spot where the Ventura Oil Field was discovered under a lemon orchard is known as the Barnard Apex. During Kinsey's childhood, Ventura was mostly agricultural and a real part of the Old West, very different than Ventura today. Every day after school Kinsey would run to the barn, saddle up her horse and ride away to pretend she was Annie Oakley, tracking rustlers through the hills.

Kinsey's father liked shooting, and so he probably met Clark at either the exclusive and private La Grulla Gun Club in Baja or the Port Hueneme Duck Club near Oxnard in Ventura County. However, at that time no women were allowed at the latter club and Clark liked to shoot with his wives, so this may have been the reason why he co-founded the Club Patos Al Viento with Ray Barnard, Barron Hilton and his associate Ray Holmes.

Clark and Kathleen would often arrive to stay with the Barnard family during duck hunting season in the fall. Kinsey was too young then to know that Clark was an important movie star, but she recognized him as a very special man as soon as they met and was always excited to see him again. She remembers him as tall and good-looking with a smile that-

155   At the Club Patos Al Viento, Clark lights the cigarette of Kinsey Barnard's father Ray G. Barnard, with Barron Hilton's associate Ray Holmes perched opposite (courtesy Kinsey Barnard).

stretched from one famous ear to the other. Best of all, he was always very kind to her. Kinsey's most vivid Gable memory is of the day she found his lost car keys. Everybody had searched for an hour trying to find those keys. When she brought them to him, he smiled and said she was his hero. "Well," she recalls, "I may have only been eight but I'm sure I must have swooned. Even at that tender age I knew that was the kind of man I hoped to marry!"

About a year later, *Run Silent Run Deep* had been released and the adults decided one night that it would be a great idea if her older sister would take the kids to see the movie and get them out from underfoot. As it happens, this is one of the very rare films in which Gable dies and, being a film about submarines, he is of course ceremonially buried at sea. Kinsey clearly saw what to her looked like dear Mr. Gable's body sliding over the side and into the water, and so she wasn't very happy on the drive back at all.

When they arrived home, the adults were having cocktails. This house had been built by screen actors Rod La Rocque and his wife Vilma Banky in the 1920s as their weekend retreat, and legend had it that it was right here at the house bar where La Rocque invented the dry martini with a twist. Consequently, Kinsey's parents felt there was a tradition to live up to, so down one side of the courtyard in the middle of the Spanish-style house was the euphemistically named "playroom" with its huge copper bar. When Kinsey and the other children entered the room, there to her utter amazement was her Mr. Gable, whom she had just seen being buried at sea, alive and well and standing behind the bar! The shock took a while to wear off, and so to help her Gable sat them down and shared stories about the making of the film, much to their delight, including how hard it had been to get his "body" to sink after they slid it into the sea.

"I often wish I had been older when I knew him," Kinsey says, "but I am so grateful to have had the opportunity to know him at all. He was more than a celebrity; he was a great person, elegant, down to earth and humble in his way. I think that, although he was the King of Hollywood, he mostly played himself; so, if you would like to know Clark Gable, just watch his movies."

156 This trio had at least three things in common: They all loved horses, they were all connected to Hollywood in some way and they had all, at one time or another, played polo. Perkins was still playing it when this photo was taken, and that latter interest was what had brought them all here to the Beverly Hills Polo Club on a fine Sunday afternoon after a polo game. Given that those in the stands frequently included such Hollywood heavyweights as Walt Disney and Darryl Zanuck, screenwriter Sy Bartlett, and actors such as Spencer Tracy, Bing Crosby and Gable, mingling with the crowd in the club house after the game and doing a little of what these days would be called "networking" never did any harm.

The talented, but often controversial, Peter Perkins grew up in California learning polo from his father Arthur, who was a star player at the Riviera and an associate of movie mogul Hal Roach, one of the founders of the Santa Anita track. By the later thirties, Peter was playing frequently at the Uplifters Club in Santa Monica with Michael Curtiz, Darryl Zanuck and Hayden Roark. Unfortunately, a few years later while he was a polo-playing resident of the Philippines, World War II broke out in the Pacific and he suddenly found himself in the army as a second lieutenant covering MacArthur's retreat. Forced with other servicemen to eat their mules when food ran out, he became a prisoner of war for over three years. He survived both the Bataan Death March and the sinking of the transport ship taking him to Japan, from where he was not to be released until war's end in 1945.

He resumed his polo career after the war, playing on several national championship teams, including the winners of the U.S. Open in 1948 and 1951. After his father introduced arena polo to Hawaii, Perkins moved there in 1952 and was often said to be the world's best arena polo player at the time. He later played international polo in England and France, riding a chestnut thoroughbred named Muntaj, and then Argentina. In 1966, he and his wife founded the San Francisco de Pilar horse farm near Buenos Aires, Argentina.

Returning to America, Perkins started Wimborne, a horse farm in Paris, Kentucky, and he became a trainer. In 1985 he teamed with Willy Shoemaker to win the Santa Anita Handicap with Lord of War in front of a crowd of 85,527 — the largest in the history of the track. That horse went on to win five other stakes on dirt and grass in California, finishing with 10 victories in 17 starts earning over $789,000. Perkins passed away in 1996, aged 78, in Del Rey Beach, Florida.

Martha Crawford-Cantarini's stepfather, Carl Crawford, was also a professional polo player who taught her how to ride and play polo when she was young. He also coached, played and socialized with prominent members of Hollywood society, and so she grew up with child actors such as Shirley Temple, Mickey Rooney, and Judy Garland. She became one of the top show riders of hunters and jumpers in California, but she dearly wanted to ride in the movies instead.

Eventually given a contract, she became the regular stunt double for such well-known actors as Eleanor Parker (to whom Martha bore a remarkable resemblance), Anne Baxter, Claudette Colbert, Lana Turner, Debra Paget, Carroll Baker and Shirley MacLaine in such famous movies of the '50s as *The Big Country, Interrupted Melody, Love Me Tender, The Rains of Ranchipur,* and *The Seventh Sin.* Martha also worked with three of the great stunt horse stars of the era: Ski, a famous rearing horse; Midnight, a Western movie horse star ridden by

156 Clark, Martha Crawford-Cantarini, and international polo player Peter Perkins at the Beverly Hills Polo Club in 1949 (courtesy Martha Crawford Cantarini).

such actors as Audie Murphy, Clint Eastwood and Henry Fonda; and Jim, the double for Flicka in the television series *My Friend Flicka*.

Martha worked with horses that were trained to specialize in particular stunt areas such as to fall, rear, drag, chase, jump, or to pull buggies, buckboards or coaches. By the fifties, animal stunt work in movies was being supervised by the SPCA so that casualties were being kept to a minimum, but even so Martha was saddened to see some actors treating their horses badly and objected to such unnecessarily harsh handling. She narrowly avoided being injured a number of times because of directors misunderstanding a horse's capabilities and ordering riders into potentially dangerous situations. Over the years, Martha would be responsible for rescuing a number of injured horses from movie ranches and racetracks and retiring them to her own ranch to be healed and given a new lease on life. "I let the horses be my teachers," she says. "I have always found that as we strive to learn the best ways to motivate our horses, in reality, they motivate us to be the best that we can be."

When the major studios and their memorable western films were being phased out, Martha returned to showing horses. For 12 months she had a live TV program in Las Vegas with her own palomino horse Frosted Sundae, known as "Frosty the Masked Horse," that she had raised and trained from a baby. Frosty became renowned as the "gambling horse" after rolling a seven at the craps table in the Thunderbird Casino in October 1963. He and Martha made many personal appearances together and did numerous live TV commercials.

When her husband John Cantarini, formerly one of the top jockeys in California, was badly injured in a devastating car wreck, Martha encouraged him out of a long, life-threatening coma and then slowly nursed him back to health over a number of years, using techniques she had learned from working with injured animals.

In 2004, Martha was accepted into the Stuntmen's Hall of Fame, and in 2005 she became the third stuntwoman to be honored with the Golden Boot Award. Martha was a consultant to Laura Hillenbrand for her book *Seabiscuit*, and she has now published her own memoir, *Fall Girl: My Life as a Western Stunt Double*.

Martha and Clark would meet again, in 1956, when she doubled for Eleanor Parker in the film *The King and Four Queens*. Clark commented that she reminded him of his friend Virginia Grey, and Martha reminded him of their meeting a few years before when this photo was taken. After that, they spent a lot of time in between scenes talking horses and reminiscing about polo. "What I remember most about him," Martha recalls, "was his great love of life."

157–159   The cast for *Teacher's Pet* was boosted by the addition of 67 real-life working newspaper columnists and journalists from all over the U.S. who were invited to play themselves in some scenes. Of course, this clever idea also guaranteed that the movie would receive lots of free publicity and column space.

A year later, Clark and Kathleen arrived in Cleveland while on a promotional tour for the film. After experiencing the hysteria of crowds during the thirties, including those attending *Gone with the Wind* premieres, Clark had preferred to no longer be involved with this type of event after he returned from the war, especially as Carole wasn't with him. Instead, he would often delegate Jean Garceau to appear on his behalf and then phone in her report to him. But after he and Kathleen married, she began to encourage him to be seen more in public, and they had attended the March 1958 premiere of *Teacher's Pet* together.

Now, with the additional encouragement of director George Seaton and producer William Perlberg, here they were on the publicity tour for the film. Some of the journalists who had appeared in the film were to be brought together at a press conference and reception in Cleveland. Miles Welter, amusement editor of the Ohio State University paper *Lantern*, thought it would be great publicity to try for a photo of Clark reading the paper. So, he duly managed to get himself and his fiancée, journalism student Christi Galvin, invited to the reception.

157   Christi Galvin, journalist for the Ohio State University *Lantern*, as she appeared in 1958 when she met Clark Gable (courtesy Christina Welter).

When Perlberg saw her there, he was so impressed by her close resemblance to actor Jean Peters, who incidentally had also been an Ohio State student, that he offered Christi a

158   Neither *Teacher's Pet* producer William Perlberg nor Clark can take their eyes off Christi Galvin at the Cleveland press conference for the movie in April 1958.

159   Perlberg and Clark finally decide to take a closer look at the *Lantern* with Christi (both photographs courtesy Christina Welter).

screen test if she came out to Hollywood. However, Christi was determined to become a journalist and she was explaining this to Perlberg when Clark came into the room with Kathleen on his arm. Glancing in Christi's direction, he seemed to understand the drift of the conversation and quickly made his way over to talk to her. Taking her hand in his with that famous dimpled smile, he began to ask her some questions. Like many others had felt, it seemed to her she was suddenly the only one in the room. Looking into her eyes, Clark assured her that she would really like it in Hollywood. She still remembers that his eyes "were so kind. At my age, he seemed a much older man, but still handsome and charismatic, someone with whom I felt safe. I knew immediately why women fell in love with him."

Nevertheless, Christi held out and declared that she really wanted to be a reporter. Clark smiled again, leaned down and whispered: "You're an egghead." She thought he might be making fun of her, but he said that when she saw the movie she would understand. Then, he was gone. Later, when Christi finally saw *Teacher's Pet*, she realized that Clark had given her the nickname he used for Doris Day in the film: a term for a journalist with ethics and commitment.

Christi is still writing.

160 Violet Parkhurst remembered her meeting with Clark and the subsequent occasional lunch and dinner dates with him over some four years for the rest of her long life. That magazine in their hands was not just a prop; she was interviewing Clark in order to write an article that would appear in a future issue. When Violet first met Clark, she had no idea he had been a child musician, and so she was pleasantly surprised to discover they had much in common with their enjoyment and knowledge of music and the arts. Unlike many other women

160 Artist and journalist Violet Parkhurst interviewing Clark for the South American movie magazine *Marilena*. He is in uniform for the movie *Command Decision* (with permission from Parkhurst Art Galleries).

Clark met, Violet had no desire to appear in movies; she was quite happy to know him just for who he was. Besides, she had already found her true vocation: painting. However, her house and studio in Topanga Canyon was tiny. After visiting it one day, Clark showed his appreciation of Violet's friendship and artistic ability by presenting her with a larger one in Malibu.

Having shown an early interest in painting and drawing while being raised in New England, Violet had attended the School of Practical Arts in Boston. She then won a scholarship to the Museum of Fine Arts in Rio de Janeiro, but when her ship arrived at Natal in Brazil in the late 1940s it was commandeered by the army who were fighting a revolution. Having fallen for a handsome Brazilian, Violet decided to rent a house and stay there. She learned the language, traveled along the Amazon and wrote about her experiences while also painting and drawing.

When she did return home, life seemed just a little tame after all that adventure. Besides, she wanted to finish studying art in Rio, and so she began saving money. Eventually she met a Brazilian newspaperman who suggested that, because she was fluent in Portuguese, she write and illustrate a book about her experiences using her notes and drawings. *Jaguar by the Tale* was published in Brazil with great success. Using her royalties, Violet bought a 28-foot sailboat and planned to sail it back to Brazil, but when she got as far as the Panama Canal she wasn't allowed through; the boat had to be loaded on a larger ship traveling through the Canal and they were all full. Reluctantly, she decided this would have to be the end of this voyage and so she sold her boat, but it was the beginning of her great passion for the sea and of many other voyages.

As a result of her book's popularity, three South American magazines asked Violet if she would become their foreign Hollywood correspondent. The only catch was that she would have to become a blonde because they thought she looked too "Brazilian." Well, after she tried it, Violet decided she liked the look, and thereafter she remained a blonde. Besides, she once said, she also found that as a blonde she could finally catch the guys who had merely liked her as a brunette. As a correspondent, Violet interviewed a number of Hollywood actors, including a young man by the name of Ronald Reagan who became a good friend. She found that, much like Clark, he was also a man who never forgot a favor. Not only did some of Violet's paintings end up in his personal collection, as well as in the collections of three other former American presidents, but she was invited to the dedication of the Ronald Reagan Library.

Painting was always Violet's real love; she found expression for her love of the sea in passionate, evocative seascapes in oils for which, along with her male and female nudes, she became renowned throughout America and eventually the world. Two of her seascapes were chosen with 24 works by other painters to tour Europe for the World American Cultural Exchange, including exhibitions at the Louvre and Prado, and they are now in the permanent collection of the Stockholm Museum. Other paintings can be seen in eight museums worldwide. In 2002 she was invited to China, where she was honored as the first western artist to have works hung in the Great Hall of the People's Republic and in the China National Museum of Fine Arts, and the first to present her work to a Chinese president, Hu Jintao, followed later by President Jiang Zemin. In 2005, the City of Los Angeles declared November 3 their annual Violet Parkhurst Day.

161–162   The photographer who took this photo was lucky to have Clark in his viewfinder. Not only was this one of the rare premieres Clark attended during the years between Carole Lombard's death and his marriage to Kathleen, but it occurred in the brief interval between when Lady Sylvia sued for divorce and when Clark left town to establish residence in Nevada. Hollywood has always been a small town, and being seen in public right in the middle of this

161-162 *Above and below:* Photographed by Carle, Clark meets two unknown women at the MGM premiere of *Showboat* at the Egyptian Theatre on July 17, 1951 (courtesy the Gable Archive).

domestic turmoil would have been just about the last thing Clark felt like doing. So, for some reason, it must have been important for him to be here.

The very successful gala premiere for *Showboat* was held at the Egyptian Theatre on Hollywood Boulevard on the warm summer night of July 17, 1951. Edwin Schallert observed in the *Los Angeles Times* the next day that the event "caused a stir in Hollywood last night such as has not been seen since the good old days." It was a revival of the old-fashioned, red-carpet, star-laden premieres with a warm and responsive audience that "glowed and glittered with movie-town celebrities." Apart from Clark, other iconic film figures in the audience that night included Norma Shearer, Joan Crawford, Alan Ladd, Ava Gardner and Frank Sinatra, Tony Curtis and Janet Leigh, and Irene Dunne who had starred as Magnolia in the 1936 screen version of *Showboat*.

This was in fact the third screen version of the 1926 novel written by well-known playwright and Pulitzer Prize–winning novelist Edna Ferber, whose work includes *Cimarron, Giant* and *Dinner at Eight*. The following year, Oscar Hammerstein II and Jerome Kern re-wrote it as a stage musical. Universal were the first to film it in 1929, followed by their 1936 remake directed by James Whale featuring Dunne, Allan Jones, Paul Robeson, Queenie Smith, and Hattie McDaniel. MGM tackled the 1951 update directed by George Sidney and starring Kathryn Grayson, Howard Keel, Ava Gardner and William Warfield. While they retained much of the original music, the studio changed the order of some songs, dropped most of Hammerstein's dialogue and added scenes of their own. Debate has raged since then over comparisons between the 1936 and 1951 film versions and the play.

Still, that was in the future from this summer night in Los Angeles on which Clark looks as if he's really enjoying himself.

163 It was the film *Never Let Me Go*, in which Gene Tierney plays a Russian ballerina and Clark an American foreign correspondent who smuggles her out of the country, that brought Clark and Tierney together to form their friendship. By the time they met, the svelte and hauntingly beautiful Tierney was a household name due to her performances in *Leave Her to Heaven* and *Laura* and rumored romances with Oleg Cassini, Howard Hughes, and Jack Kennedy.

The lead role in *Never Let Me Go* was a very physically demanding part, requiring the 32-year-old Tierney to take two hours of ballet lessons every day for six weeks before and during the shoot. Her feet swelled and blistered, and the considerate Clark took to bringing back a specially-made salve ointment for her from Paris, to which he'd fly whenever he had a few days break.

Tierney's mother dearly wanted her and Clark to become an item but Tierney was bothered by the 20-year age gap. Nevertheless, they often went out for dinner and found they had much to talk about. She, too, always remembered him as a sweet man who still talked a lot about Carole and who, for all his tough he-man image, was happy to reveal to her his real gentleness.

163 Clark and Gene Tierney looking relaxed together while on a break from shooting *Never Let Me Go* in England in July 1952 (courtesy the Gable Archive).

164–165 Jean Garceau started out as Carole's personal assistant in October 1938, had taken on the same job for both the Gables after their marriage, and then continued working in that capacity for Clark after Carole's death. She kept track of personal income, of banking and investment, bill payments, accounts and tax statements. She hired and fired the house and ranch staff, looked after travel arrangements and appointments, and sorted and then answered the mail after Clark and Carole had read it.

It might sound trivial, but mail was no small operation for a star couple as popular as Carole and Clark. Some of it could be a trifle edgy; Jean maintained what she called a "mad woman" file in Clark's case to head off at the pass any potential threats to personal safety and solicitations of both money and affection. Although MGM also had a mail department, piles of it still arrived at the house and the genuine fan mail had to be sorted from the rest.

164 Photographed in an unlikely situation, as he hated dictating and she typed badly, are Clark and his executive assistant of many years, Jean Garceau (courtesy Carole Sampeck/Carole Lombard Archive).

EMITTANCE FROM CLARK GABLE

	DESCRIPTION		ACCOUNT	AMOUNT
	RECEIVED FROM JEAN GARCEAU THE FOLLWOING MONEY			
	Clark Gable			
	ALLWOANCE FOR CLARK GABLE			
	MONTH OF JUNE		401	1,000 00

W. RITTER CO. 80879   DETACH STATEMENT BEFORE DEPOSITING

165 As can be seen from this check, Jean really did type badly and The King was on an allowance (courtesy Carole Sampeck/Carole Lombard Archive).

166 Clark in Palm Springs at the end of March 1960 (courtesy the Gable Archive).

People would send gifts such as pipes, bookends, handkerchiefs and clocks for which Jean would write a "thank you" letter, after which they were usually given to charity.

She had originally worked for the Myron Selznick agency where she had been Carole's contact person. She always spoke fondly of the folks she worked with at the agency, particularly the charming William Powell who had a holiday tradition of setting up a bar in the agency office called "Willie Poo's."

Her predecessor as Carole's personal assistant had been Madalynne Fields, or "Fieldsie" as she was often known, Carole's manager, alter ego, close friend and roommate. Jean was offered her job when Fieldsie married film director Walter Lang. Despite some initial hesitation, she moved into the office in Carole's Tudor-style house on St. Cloud Road. It was there she first met Clark Gable in 1938 when Carole began coaching him in chorus-line dance steps for his role in *Idiot's Delight*. She immediately decided she liked Clark when she asked if he was looking forward to playing Rhett Butler and he admitted he was scared to death.

It was Jean who helped Carole find and settle on Raoul Walsh's ranch in Encino, with its two-story Connecticut farmhouse, split-rail fences and stables for nine horses, when she and Clark were searching for a home. When they moved in, Clark and Carole set up an office for her. Decorated in yellow and blue, it became the nerve center of the Gable household and of their business and studio affairs. They called her "Jeanie" and treated her as one of the family, but for her Clark was always "Mr. G." She became such an intimate friend that it was to her Carole entrusted a set of notes that she'd written for Clark to be opened, one day at a time, while she was away on her last trip.

Jeanie continued to manage the Encino ranch property while Clark was with the Air Force during World War II and then while he traveled overseas on film shoots during subsequent years. She was the first he called when Lady Sylvia agreed to marry him. Because Sylvia brought her own house staff with her, Clark at first built Jean an office at her own home but, as that didn't work out, he built a guest house on the ranch property and moved Jean's office back into there.

After Clark returned from working on *But Not for Me* in 1959, Jean finally decided to retire. After 20 years with the Gable family, it was a hard move to make even though she had been thinking it over for some time. Clark had kept pleading that no one else could do the job as well as she, but now that he was involved in a wonderful marriage and had a good agent, Jean felt that it was time to reclaim her own life. Besides, the relationship between her and Kathleen was becoming increasingly uncomfortable. Perhaps Jean reminded her too much of Clark's marriage to Carole, or perhaps Kathleen preferred to have her own staff, but the personal situation between the two women was not working out and Jeanie felt it was time to move on. Her memories of her life with the Gables became part of her book *Dear Mr. G*.

After her husband Russel passed away in 1981, Jean sold their Los Angeles house and moved to a retirement village near San Francisco. She continued to lead an active life, traveling a great deal and even taking a hot air balloon ride across France. She died in 1985.

166   Less than eight months before his death, and only six weeks before starting work on his final film *The Misfits*, Clark had lost 30 pounds in preparation for his role as a horse wrangler. Kathleen and Clark had settled into their new Bermuda Dunes house, where they had stayed during winter and into spring, and Clark was taking his golf game so seriously that he was hitting in the high seventies. He was looking and feeling better than he had for years.

Married Life

167 For many years, Clark erased Josephine from his life so completely that many people didn't even know she had been the first Mrs. Gable. To this day, no one really knows the personal details of their marriage. Josephine loved Clark and certainly respected him far too much to ever give away many personal secrets.

Born in 1884, and thus 17 years older than Clark, Josephine was a slight, gentle, determined, well-educated and industrious woman with dark brown hair and hazel eyes from a large Southern Californian family who lived on a 40-acre ranch. Her four sisters were singers, composers and artists; her father, Henry Clay Dillon (1846–1912), was an early supporter of women's suffrage, the Los Angeles County district attorney from 1892 to 1894 and a Los Angeles Superior Court commissioner before he exchanged a career in law for one in oil. Josephine graduated from Stanford University in 1908, when few women had done so, studied theater in Italy, became a well-known actor in New York and had traveled to Turkey with the American Committee for Armenian and Syrian Relief before deciding to take up teaching voice and stage technique.

A friend who had moved to Portland, Oregon, to teach subsequently sent back glowing reports and so, perhaps tired of big city living, Josephine too moved across the country to Portland, rented a large house and converted the lower floor to a theater studio. Before long, she had established the Little Theatre and was already known in the area when Clark joined her group to study the stage.

They quickly established a mutual relationship of driving ambition. With a lot of imagination and more than enough faith in himself, Clark wanted to learn everything that would provide him with an escape from odd jobs and poverty, and he immediately saw that Josephine had the experience and connections to help him become a successful actor. Josephine in turn recognized that Clark had more potential to be an actor than any of her students; she just wasn't sure at first that he was teachable. In all probability, Josephine didn't count on falling for the younger Clark as part of the deal, but perhaps because they spent so much time working closely together she apparently did just that.

After about a year of training Clark in theatrical technique, and obviously deeply emotionally involved with him by now, Josephine made the huge decision in the summer of 1924 to close her studio and move them both to Los Angeles where she knew there would be more opportunity for Clark's career. After they married in December, Josephine continued to devotedly teach drama and support him morally and financially while he found only bit parts in

167 A young and elegant Josephine Dillon photographed well before meeting Clark (courtesy the Gable Archive).

silent movies; she trained him how to stand, walk fluently, breathe correctly and lower his voice pitch. The following year, Clark successfully auditioned for the team of theater producer Louis O. Macloon and his wife, director Lillian Albertson. He never looked back, playing increasingly more important roles in a number of their touring productions over the following five years.

Once he had stepped onto the first rungs of the ladder of fame, Clark evidently didn't look back for Josephine, either. Touring took him away from home for long periods and he had already been seen in the company of some notable female actors such as Jane Cowl and Pauline Frederick by the time he and Josephine quietly separated at the end of 1926. By early 1929, with Clark openly planning his next marriage to Ria Prentiss Langham, Josephine decided she couldn't take it any more and applied for a divorce on March 28 on grounds of desertion. Clark didn't contest, and the final divorce decree was granted the following year on April 1.

For the rest of her life, Josephine could never quite emerge from Clark's shadow. On the one hand, she claimed she didn't want people to always think of her just as Clark Gable's first wife, but as an independent woman in her own right. Yet, on the other hand, she couldn't seem to entirely let the association be forgotten, either. She had, after all, changed the path of her life for him and to entirely erase him would make that meaningless. So, like some Ancient Mariner of Hollywood, she could not resist an opportunity to remind people who she was and tell her tale. In 1933, for example, she published two "Open Letters to Clark Gable from his Former Wife" in the magazine *Motion Picture* criticizing his voice and his acting style, urging him to present more of the character and less of Clark Gable. It only served to annoy Clark enough for him to stop her maintenance payments, which were being made under a confidentiality agreement.

Much like poor Franz Dorfler, Clark barely mentioned Josephine's name again. When asked how he came to be an actor, he would just grin and shrug and say he'd got lucky. Josephine, who didn't seem to mind mentioning Clark, remained a well-known stage director, teacher and acting coach with her own studio in Los Angeles for many years; her lengthy student list included names such as Gary Cooper, Nelson Eddy and Bruce Cabot. In 1940 her book *Modern Acting: A Guide for Stage, Screen and Television* was published, becoming a respected text that is still referred to today.

However, in 1956 a story appeared in *Confidential* magazine in which Josephine apparently claimed she was in financial difficulties because Clark, who had never supported her, didn't care about her situation. Public reaction was intense; her students left and her coaching business was practically wiped out overnight. The following year, she appeared as one of the witnesses in the famous *Confidential* libel trial to say that the stories had been a complete fabrication and that now she was totally dependant on Social Security as a result of the reaction to them.

True to form, when he learned about what had really happened, Clark purchased the title for her house at 12746 Landale, North Hollywood, to make sure she would be able to keep it and he left provision in his will ensuring Josephine retained perpetual title. When the media arrived at her door after his death, Josephine could for a brief moment, photograph of the young actor in hand, once more claim her fame as the woman who had "created" Clark Gable. Unfortunately, she wasn't even allowed her memories in peace: those interviews and the appearance of her name in Gable biographies the following year led to the 78-year-old woman receiving hate mail and threatening phone calls. Asked at one time why she never remarried, Josephine quipped that she had thought about it several times, but had then considered "how unfair it would be to any man to go through life known as the fellow who married Clark Gable's first wife."

168 If Josephine taught Clark about the stage, then Ria taught him about living well, about what life was like with money and connections. Ironically the same age as Josephine, this woman had a lot more life experience; Ria had already been married three times and was a mother with two children when she met Clark. In fact, it was through one of the children that they first encountered one another.

From late 1927 through the spring of 1928, Clark was playing on stage at Houston's Palace Theatre as part of Gene Lewis' stock company and then with the Laskin Brothers. Many of the young ladies of the town became quite Gable-struck during his stay; one who went to see Clark and sigh was a 14-year-old redhead by the name of George Anna Lucas, who preferred to be called Jana. She and her friend had a terrible crush on him but she didn't want her mother Ria Langham, with whom she was close, to know about it. Jana and her mother were so close, in fact, that she was always sure Ria never met Clark in Houston. That fateful meeting would wait until later in 1928 after Ria had moved to New York when her eldest boy, who had been in school in Connecticut, fell ill and needed the best medical treatment. Jana had graduated from school, so she moved with them into a luxurious apartment on 81st and Park Avenue in Manhattan.

Ria (Maria) Franklin Prentiss Lucas Langham was a petite, strong-minded woman with exquisite taste and a fine sense of proprieties. She was a lady with style and she taught Clark as much about it as she could. Her first marriage at 17 to William Prentiss, with whom she had a son, fell apart within four years. By then her mother had died and her father and his new wife had moved to Texas, so Ria moved from Illinois to Houston where she found work in Lechenger's Jewelry Store. Into that store, one day in early 1910, walked prosperous builder and widower Alfred Lucas, and her life changed. By May they were married and she was in charge of a mansion and three children. Their own first child was George Anna in 1913 and then six years later there was Alfred Jr. before Alfred Sr. died in 1922. Two years later she married Daniel Langham; two years after that, they divorced. Four years later, she married Clark.

Ria and Clark were probably married in New York very shortly after his divorce came through, and the time period may have been too short. Evidently, 12 months later someone pointed out to Howard Strickling, the head of public relations at MGM, that the Gable marriage wasn't actually legal in California. For some reason, Clark picked the Santa Ana courthouse to correct the mistake and tie the knot all over again on June 19, 1931. The location was a customary Hollywood marriage altar and the press had it well staked out, descending on the pair when they arrived. Ria was so shaken by her first encounter with that level of media attention that she never spoke publicly to the press again.

168 Ria Langham Gable and Clark attending a social function (courtesy the Gable Archive).

169 For quite some time, Clark tried to be the elegantly social film star that Ria wanted him to be, and they were seen at important Hollywood social occasions such as this one. Directed by Frank Lloyd for the Fox Film Corporation, *Cavalcade* was based on the very successful Noël Coward play and went on to win three Academy Awards: Best Picture, Best Director and Best Art Direction. Una O'Connor, Irene Brown and Merle Tottenham reprised

169 Clark and Ria attend the West Coast premiere of *Cavalcade* at the Chinese Theatre in Hollywood with Helen Hayes and her husband Charles MacArthur on January 12, 1933 (courtesy the Gable Archive).

their stage roles in this film about the lives of two British families during the first 33 years of the 20th century.

The tiny and elfinly beautiful Helen Hayes, five feet and 100 pounds, and the six-foot-tall Clark would be seen together much more during the year, starring together in two movies: *The White Sister*, which opened in LA on April 27, and *Night Flight*, which opened in L.A.

on October 4. Although Clark once asked her out on a date, she was too shy to accept. Having begun her stage career at age eight, Hayes became regarded as one of the three great female stage actors of the era and was still held in such high regard that all the Broadway marquee lights were dimmed for a minute on the night she died in March 1993. Hayes had already won an Academy Award for Best Actress for her first major film role in *The Sin of Madelon Claudet* (1931). Forty years later, she won a second Oscar for Best Supporting Actress in *Airport*. Raised and educated a Roman Catholic, she was denied sacraments for marrying playwright Charles MacArthur, who had divorced in order to marry her; MacArthur and Ben Hecht wrote the hit play *The Front Page*. He never recovered from the death of their daughter in 1949 and drank heavily until his death seven years later. Hayes went on to win Emmy and Tony awards and have two Broadway theaters named after her in recognition of her contributions to theater, film and television.

Unfortunately, Ria couldn't be the type of woman with whom Clark was able to share his rapidly developing interest in hunting, shooting and fishing. Although she initially gave it a good try, Ria didn't like living outdoors in a tent and cooking over a campfire. She was a woman who preferred to eat from a table set with silverware and surrounded with fashionable friends. After a while Clark started to complain about having to dress for dinner after a long day's work and how much all this entertaining was costing him. However, having already been a wealthy and independent woman and mother when she married Clark, Ria didn't see why she should play second fiddle in Clark's orchestra and change her lifestyle just to suit him. One of her problems was that she could overplay the hand. She couldn't see, as Clark did, that many of their so-called "friends" only visited them to see Hollywood at home rather than real people.

Still, Ria was determined to be there for Clark as long as he needed her and, although their relationship had its problems, Clark absolutely doted on his stepchildren who in turn adored him. When Jana was old enough, he bought her a car and then paid her a regular salary, just like he would anyone else, when she went to work as his secretary. He could be over-protective just like any father, too. When she was having her portrait painted, for example, he accompanied Jana to every sitting because he didn't trust the artist. Nor did he approve of her first boyfriend, seizing a poker one night and chasing him out of the house.

As time passed, Clark and Ria found less in common. She would socialize, shop, play bridge with friends, or organize lunches and dinners while Clark worked long hours and then disappeared under the hood of a car or on a horse with a hunting rifle as soon as he was out of the studio gate. Then along came Joan Crawford, and everything became personal. In an attempt to put out the fire, MGM organized a coast-to-coast publicity tour for the Gable family, and Mayer personally ordered Joan and Clark to quit their relationship at the risk of losing their jobs. For a while things seemed to settle down, but the rumors didn't. At least one rumor in the shape of Loretta Young would in time prove correct. When Clark found himself involved in the Violet Norton paternity case later in 1937, the facts of the case may have been somewhat sadly ridiculous, but hardly anyone was surprised about its subject. By the time Carole Lombard came along and put poor Ria out of her misery, she and Clark were no longer living together.

Ironically, Ria's divorce from Clark in 1939 unintentionally publicized the quick Las Vegas divorce. Although Nevada had changed its laws in 1931 enabling the granting of a divorce upon proof of six weeks residency, it would be the national headlines of the Gable divorce that started the boom. Ria arrived in Vegas on January 20, 1939, and set up residence for the required period. Clark remained back in California, busy with his involvement with Carole and with working on *Gone with the Wind*. The ever well-mannered Ria sued for divorce on

170　Carole with her dachshunds some time before she met Clark (courtesy the Gable Archive).

the grounds that Clark had deserted her and their home as far back as 1935 because he wanted more freedom, not on grounds of his affairs with either Joan or Carole. Dressed for the occasion in a black and pink wool suit and tall black pagoda-style straw hat, she was granted her divorce after a five-minute hearing on March 7, 1939. Ria became the first Vegas celebrity divorcee, probably gaining more media attention as she left the marriage than she had during it.

170–171　Unlike Clark's previous two wives, Carole Lombard was a recognized film star celebrity in her own right before he met her. Only a few years younger, Carole had her own career at Paramount where she was not far from being Clark's equivalent in star value. She had an independent income, her own property, her own fans and could stand up for herself. Not only that, she wasn't in awe of him; she liked practical jokes as much as Clark did and she was quite up to teasing him if he became too full of himself. Clark had never really known what it was like to have a lasting and meaningful relationship with a woman who was his peer, and Carole would give him that chance. A beautiful woman who could express her own mind very directly, she was entirely Clark's equal and that was a different situation for him.

　　Maybe, too, they were both in just the right place in their lives for that relationship when

171 A magazine advertisement from 1941 featuring Carole extolling the virtues of Lux Soap (courtesy the Gable Archive).

they danced together at the White Mayfair Ball on the night of January 26, 1936, and seemed to realize that there might be more to their friendship. They were obviously not in that place four years previously when they met on the set of *No Man of Her Own*. For one thing, they were both very much married at that time, Carole to William Powell and Clark to Ria. No sparks had immediately ignited but they established a friendship which they maintained over the years. Now their situations were somewhat different, and when they met again on February 7 at Jock Whitney's party, they felt able to become involved with each other.

Jane Alice Peters, as Carole was born, had been abruptly moved from her hometown of Fort Wayne, Indiana, at the age of seven when her parents divorced and her mother took her and her two older brothers to live in Los Angeles. They grew up a close family, with Jane developing a tough competitive edge as she fought to stay equal with her brothers, playing football and

172   Looking a long way from a Lux Soap advertisement, Carole is photographed by Clark squinting into the sun during a hunting trip (courtesy the Gable Archive).

baseball, swimming and winning medals in track and field. Her feisty personality caught the attention of director Allan Dwan who, while visiting neighbors by the name of Lombard, caught sight of the 12-year-old next door boxing with her brothers and cast her in her first movie.

That initial experience gave her a goal. After graduating from high school, she was enrolled in drama school and then when she turned 16 was put under contract to the Fox studio and began appearing in movies. Carol borrowed the name Lombard from those past neighbors, and the story goes that her mother consulted numerology for advice about adding the "e" at the end of her daughter's name. However, it's quite possible that the spelling change came about simply because Fox accidentally spelled it as Carole on an early film credit and the future star retained it as a good-luck omen.

Nevertheless, good luck seemed to be absent when she was thrown through the windshield of a car in an accident in 1926 and received facial injuries. Fortunately she recovered and was able to return to work, this time appearing in slapstick comedies for the Mack Sennett studio. After they closed, she moved to Pathé and then in 1930 negotiated a five-year contract with Paramount. While making *Man of the World* there with William Powell, they fell in love and

173 Clark and Carole happily sitting on the tailgate of their Woody Wagon (courtesy the Gable Archive).

married in 1931. They were a wealthy, elegant couple but Powell was 16 years older, rarely stepped out of his movie character persona and didn't approve of her blue vocabulary.

So, when they met during *No Man of Her Own*, Carole and Clark were both rather preoccupied with relationship problems. It was unfortunate in a way; this was the only film they would ever make together. Still, by the time the shoot wrapped, they had come to know each

174   Carole captures Clark on film with Nan and Harry Fleischmann at their Bakersfield gun club, October 1939 (courtesy the Gable Archive).

175   In turn, Clark photographs a rather bored Carole with an adoring Nan Fleischmann (courtesy the Gable Archive).

other well enough to exchange aptly tongue-in-cheek gifts: She presented him with a big ham with his picture on it and he presented her with some fluffy ballet slippers into which he thought she might grow.

172–173   While they certainly loved each other, there's no doubt that Carole saw the same advantages in becoming Mrs. Clark Gable as any other red-blooded young woman at the time. Seizing the opportunity with which fate presented her, Carole set out to be just the sort of woman whom Clark would want to have around. Well aware of Ria's shortcomings when it came to Gable relationships, the highly intelligent Carole would have determined she would not

176 Clark and Carole in conversation with Garson Kanin, probably at the time he was directing Carole in mid–1940 at RKO in *They Knew What They Wanted* (courtesy the Gable Archive).

make the same mistakes. She would become the woman whom Clark would not want to leave at home.

So, she had the young Robert Stack give her shooting lessons and quickly proved she had a sharp eye that would definitely give Clark a contest when it came to skeet and ducks. Clark taught her to fish, and she was right there alongside him whenever they retreated to his favorite Rogue River place.

174–175 As well as having owned the Los Angeles–Santa Monica Gun Club, Harry and Nan Fleischmann owned a duck club south of Bakersfield, California, and Clark and Carole came to spend so much time there that the Fleischmanns built them a cabin, the interior of which you can see in these photos. Carole liked to quip that she furnished it in Early Sears Roebuck. The two couples became close friends and would often drive down together to the La Grulla Gun Club, south of the Mexican border near Ensenada.

Harry died unexpectedly of a heart attack in November 1943. Clark and Jeannie drove up for the funeral, for they had all remained close after Carole's death. When Nan decided to sell the lodge a year later, Clark was saddened all over again as the place had come to mean a great deal to him. Some of his hunting friends urged him to buy it, but his Encino home

177 Photographed by Clark, Carole looks pensive at the La Grulla Gun Club in Mexico in 1939 (courtesy the Gable Archive).

was the only real estate Clark was truly interested in and so he declined. Clark maintained his friendship with Nan after she moved to Pacific Palisades; because she knew him so well, Clark always trusted that Nan would have a frank opinion.

176 Twenty-four-year-old director, actor, playwright and screen writer Garson Kanin (1912–1999) arrived in Hollywood in 1937, brought from New York by Samuel Goldwyn to "learn the business." Until enlisting during World War II he worked for RKO, directing such films as *The Great Man Votes* (1939) and *My Favorite Wife* (1940). After the war, he and his wife Ruth Gordon collaborated on screenplays such as *Pat and Mike* and *Adam's Rib*. In 1950 Kanin was paid the then-record sum of $1,000,000 by Harry Cohn at Columbia for the rights to his very successful play *Born Yesterday* that he'd been directing on Broadway. After opening on February 4, 1946, it ran for 1642 performances. He also wrote the novel *Do Re Mi* from which the screenplay for *The Girl Can't Help It* (1956) was adapted.

Kanin had originally wanted to make *Cyrano de Bergerac* for RKO with two actors he'd handpicked but production chief Harry Edington preferred to use Lombard and Charles Laughton, who were already under contract, to make *They Knew What They Wanted* which they already owned. Sydney Howard had won a Pulitzer Prize for the play. Tired of a fragmented moviemaking system in which actors often didn't know why they were speaking lines, Kanin ordered all 50 cast and production crew into a rehearsal. The only person who couldn't be there was Carole, who was suffering from contact with poison oak so severely that her face was swollen to the point she couldn't eat.

Eventually she recovered enough to work, and the working relationship between her and Kanin developed into a friendship. Kanin couldn't fail to be impressed by a female actor of that era whose normal style of speech was liberally sprinkled with "fuck," who insisted on doing her own makeup and hair on set, never fluffed a line, was never late, and memorized her marks. Everyone adored her. She would even drive in on days she was not required so she wouldn't lose the momentum of work. Kanin thought her one of the finest natural female actors he'd ever encountered. When he once asked her about her wide range of roles, she put it down to the men with whom she'd been in relationships: with the intellectual Bob Riskin she'd read serious literature; with Russ Columbo she'd learned about music, bands, songs, songwriting and Italian cooking; with William Powell she'd learned how to be a ladylike wife and put a house together; and with Clark it was the ranch and horses and fishing and shooting.

Carole told Kanin that the first time she and Clark had realized the romantic potential of their relationship was at Jock Whitney's "all-white" party on February 7, 1936. Carole, dressed in a white hospital gown, had been driven to the party in a white ambulance and carried in by two attendants on a stretcher. Clark, who was a renowned lover of a good practical joke, was hugely impressed and asked her out on dates. On Valentine's Day, she sent him an old Model T Ford liberally plastered in red hearts in which they gaily drove off to dinner together. After that, as far as Carole was concerned, the more she knew him, the more she felt there was to know. "Clark's a wonder," she'd say. "I'm really nuts about him."

177   There were many comments about how much the previously refined Carole became the rough-and-ready Carole for Clark, but in many ways Clark changed too. She was so full of life and confidence, of love and light-hearted companionship that Clark began to shake off the fears that had tended to hover over him that this fortunate life might all vanish tomorrow. Thanks to Carole, he came to believe more in himself.

It was typical of the pragmatic and positive Carole that one of her favorite quotations, read at the funeral service of her and her mother on January 21, 1942, was the following words of the Persian philosopher Baha'u'llah: "I have made death even as glad tidings unto thee. Why dost thou mourn at its approach?"

178   Clark's marriage to Lady Sylvia Ashley Fairbanks Stanley caught everyone unawares, possibly even Clark himself. Although Clark later claimed they had known each other for two or three years, the couple had only been seen in public together for a few months and Sylvia had appeared to be just another of his close female friends. However, this lady had much more than friendship in mind.

Tall, willowy and golden-haired, with a shrewd quick wit and impeccable taste in clothes and jewelry, Sylvia was faintly similar in appearance to Carole but otherwise seemed to have more in common with Joan Crawford in the extent of her desire to better herself. The daughter of an English footman, Edith Louisa Sylvia Hawkes was born only three years after Clark. Starting work as a living mannequin in a dress-maker's shop, the tall, slim and elegant Sylvia soon earned the nickname "Silky" because long, slinky silk negligees looked so good on her. Determined to rise above the dressmaker's floor, however, the ambitious Sylvia became a Cochran Dancer, the British equivalent of a Ziegfeld Follies girl, before graduating to acting in 1924.

While appearing in a number of West End plays, her beauty caused her to stand out from the crowd and she caught the roving eye of the very rich Anthony Ashley-Cooper, Lord Ashley and son of the 9th Earl of Shaftesbury. Needless to say, the earl was not amused that his son had fallen into the arms of a commoner. Upon discovering his son had actually proposed, he refused to sanction the match but the pair scandalously eloped and duly married in 1927, only to justify the earl's fears by soon separating. They finally divorced in 1934; the substantial settlement meant that Sylvia would never again have to do any high-kicks in public, nor would she ever relinquish her title.

Finally confirming long-standing rumors, Lord Ashley named the famous actor Douglas Fairbanks, married to Mary Pickford, as co-respondent in the divorce. Having met in 1931, Sylvia and Douglas had been involved in an affair. Despite his belated protestations of love, Fairbanks was divorced by Pickford and in 1936 married Sylvia in Paris, from where they returned to live in Fairbanks' Santa Monica beach house with a huge over-sexed bull-mastiff named Marco Polo that would attempt to molest anyone who entered. Realizing it had all been a mistake, a disillusioned and tired Fairbanks passed away only three years later. Once again, Sylvia was left a wealthy woman, bequeathed some $2,000,000 in Fairbanks' will. In

178   Clark and Sylvia photographed at the Encino ranch just after their marriage in 1949 (courtesy the Gable Archive).

grief and no doubt with some gratitude, she spent $40,000 of it on her personally supervised, magnificent marble Fairbanks memorial that stands in the Hollywood Forever Cemetery. Its classical Greek symmetry is still reflected in the long pool that's sighted towards the Hollywood sign on the distant hills.

In 1944, Sylvia became the second wife of Lt. Commander Edward John Stanley, 6th Baron Sheffield, 6th Baron Stanley of Alderley and 5th Baron Eddisbury who was already developing a fondness for gambling and wine. He subsequently went to sea while she went to London and four years later he sued her for divorce on grounds of desertion. Sylvia returned to the Santa Monica house Fairbanks had left her.

No stranger to the Fairbanks family, Clark had probably known Sylvia for much longer than people were aware. They seemed to have little in common, but Clark's loneliness coupled with Sylvia's desire to maintain her social status seems to have convinced them it was all about love. Clark proposed on December 18, 1949; Sylvia agreed immediately and they were married two days later at the Alisal Ranch near Solvang, California. The very next day, Sylvia received her first taste of being Carole Lombard's successor in marriage to the "King" of Hollywood when they boarded the Matson Line ship *Lurline* at San Francisco for Hawaii. The press had advertised their departure and when they arrived on the pier with a motorcycle escort, it was to find their way blocked by hundreds of screaming women. Ten escorting police officers had to form a flying wedge to push a path through the crowd so that the Gables could board. As they were being welcomed aboard by Matson officials, the line broke and a stampeding wave of a thousand rioting women materialized out of the night and, trampling all before it, swept the Gables down corridors and into their suite on a flood tide that continued to pound on the closed doors until the Gables reluctantly gave a brief press conference. Only when the last weeping woman was led off the ship, sobbing that she could kiss Clark's feet, could the ship depart.

Four days later, Sylvia once again had to face the fact she had married a man who could cause riots, even on tropical islands. This time when they looked down from the rails of their ship, it was to discover not 1000 waiting fans but a heaving, surging mass of 10,000. It took the entire Honolulu police force to hold the crowd back and another motorcycle escort to get them off the pier. They finally retired to their rented house with private beach where they enjoyed a relaxing three-week honeymoon.

179 This was Clark and Sylvia's first film location trip together, and it seems to have been the period during which Clark and Sylvia were happiest. Her entertaining, her dogs and her aristocratic manners hadn't yet started to really irritate him. Perhaps as a way of respecting Clark's previous marriage, Sylvia did not make many changes to the Encino house apart from moving in some of her fine English antiques, her priceless rose quartz, and a stunning jewelry collection. However, she did redecorate her bedroom (which of course had previously been Carole's) in shades of pink and white; it was an unfortunate choice because pink was a color Clark detested. She planned all the menus, put in four large landscaped rose gardens, and guided the construction of a two-bedroom guest house on the property. Then Sylvia began to entertain on a lavish scale.

She did at least initially make an attempt to share his work with him, and this trip was part of that attempt. While at the Indianapolis 500, Clark was in his element surrounded by men and machines; it was very much his kind of place. His good friend Al Menasco came along with his son to watch the race, as did Sylvia's nephew Timothy Bleck. Sylvia set up a kitchen in their hotel suite and insisted on feeding everybody.

179   Clark and Sylvia at the Indianapolis 500 while Clark was there shooting *To Please a Lady* in May 1950 (courtesy Indianapolis Motor Speedway Photo Operations).

Two stories about Clark at the Indianapolis 500 say a lot about the sort of guy he was:

It was the hottest summer in years there and the hundreds of fans who stormed Clark whenever he appeared were not only insistent but panicky. A smiling Clark would stand for hours bare-headed in the heat signing anything they put in front of him, from gloves to programs. When a Speedway guard once started to push the crowd back, telling them to leave him alone, Clark told him quietly that those people were his friends who were responsible for him being where he was and to let them be.

Clark often liked to stroll through the garage area to talk with drivers and mechanics, and one day he came across some young drivers who had brought their cars from California. After talking with them a while, he discovered they weren't eating because they had put all their money into the cars. A while later they discovered their accounts at the racetrack restaurant had been mysteriously fully paid up for the time they were there.

After the shoot was over, Clark returned home while Sylvia flew to England in an attempt to straighten out some of her complicated legal affairs. By the time she arrived back in Los Angeles three weeks later, Clark and Jeanie were making preparations for a six-week stay in Durango, Colorado, which would be the location of his next movie, *Across the Wide Missouri*.

180–181 Although they still looked happy while in Durango, which really amounted to a third honeymoon for them, cracks were starting to appear in their union. It was becoming clearer as the days went by that they really had little in common, and Clark was beginning to grow restless. Try as she might, and she did, Sylvia simply could not be Carole. While Clark loved the great outdoors and a few close friends, Sylvia was devoted to the great indoors, to her long golden hair and her makeup, and was happiest at salons and tea parties. They may have laughed a lot together but when it came down to it, Clark held his money close to his chest while Sylvia liked spreading it around.

The cast made the cabins of the El Rancho Encantado in Durango their base while working on *Across the Wide Missouri*. Sylvia immediately set about turning their two-room log cabin into a home as she hung curtains, had turf laid outside the door and cooked their meals in the cabin, all of which made Clark the butt of some jokes amongst the crew. That

180 Sylvia and Clark looking fashionably Western while in Durango. Sylvia's outfit had been tailor-made in Hollywood (courtesy the Gable Archive).

didn't sit well with the man who preferred to be one of them, not apart from them, and so he and Sylvia were soon eating with everyone else at the long tables in the huge mess tent that could hold the entire company at one sitting.

Of course, Clark just couldn't resist all those mountain streams full of fish waiting for his line, and he would grab a rod and be gone the minute he was no longer needed on the set. Sylvia gave it a shot, but she really preferred to sit on the bank and paint while Clark did his thing. Every evening they would go out riding together with Clark mounted on Steel, the horse on which he is seen in the movie.

This time, with no secret romance to come between them, director William Wellman and Clark got along well. Unfortunately, MGM was apparently horrified with the hundreds of feet of lyrical, magnificently scenic, almost documentary-type material with which Wellman returned from a very expensive outdoor location shoot and consequently ordered the film pared down to 78 minutes of action sequences and vignettes. Consequently, the story seems to lack connection and to end abruptly with loose ends untied. Unfortunately, through no fault of Wellman or Clark, *Across the Wide Missouri* doesn't quite fulfill its potential.

For that matter, neither did Clark and Sylvia's marriage. Once back home, she saw less need to maintain the pretence of liking the outdoor life. When they returned in January of 1951 from Christmas in Bermuda with friends, they were no longer a happy couple. In early

181 Caught in a rare moment of natural humor, Clark and Sylvia find something hilarious about the hands they've been dealt during a break while in Durango, Colorado, for *Across the Wide Missouri* in August 1950 (courtesy the Gable Archive).

April, Clark checked into Cedars of Lebanon Hospital to have a complete physical in preparation for shooting *Lone Star* on location in Arizona. He must have put in a lot of thinking time while lying there, because he evidently came home and informed Sylvia he thought their marriage was a mistake, that he was tired of her aristocratic British airs and he wanted a divorce. He then left for Arizona.

Sylvia went back to Nassau for a few weeks, but when she returned in May it was to find she had been locked out of the Encino house. Finally admitting defeat, she sued for divorce at the Santa Monica courthouse on May 31 on grounds of mental cruelty. This time it was Clark who took advantage of Nevada's divorce laws; after work on *Lone Star* was over, he moved out of the Encino house to Glenbrook Lodge at Lake Tahoe to establish residency and six weeks later, on October 4, he duly filed for divorce. While property negotiations dragged on, he moved to the Flying M.E. Ranch near Carson City which became his official Nevada address.

Sylvia and Clark met one last time, in New York, just after his birthday in 1952. She had been hospitalized there after injuring her ankle in an accident and Clark came by to visit. They chatted away like the old friends they still were, and when he came back the next day they seemed reluctant to part. Their bitterness had faded, and they agreed to work out a property arrangement that would be fair without any further legal wrangling. On April 21, they divorced amicably.

The only one of Gable's wives to remarry, Sylvia would continue to indulge her tastes for the finer things in life by becoming Princess Sylvia in 1954 with her marriage to a Georgian nobleman, Ambassador Hotel executive, thoroughbred race-horse owner and 1930s race-car driver Prince Dimitri Djordjadze.

182 The British society publicist Lee Anderson once said about Clark and Kathleen Gable that they "always looked like newlyweds. They had a happiness few of us are fortunate to know. In their home, love filled every room, and we were all warmed by the glow." Born in Erie, Pennsylvania, Kathleen Gretchen Williams Capps de Alzaga Spreckels was in many ways the woman Carole might well have become if she had lived longer, with one or two exceptions. Kathleen was not a major film personality but a successful model who had appeared in one major role in the film *The Actress* (1953), after a series of largely uncredited bit parts during the 1940s. She did not have Carole's earthy turn of phrase and outlook on life.

Although other people called her Kay, Clark always called her Kathleen and they had in fact first met and become friends back in the mid–40s, many years before they married. At that time, though, they didn't seem

182 An autographed photograph of Kathleen Williams as she appeared during the 1940s while a young actor in Hollywood (courtesy the Gable Archive).

to light up the room together; evidently, as Kathleen would sagely observe later, Fate decreed they needed a little more time. So much time, as it turned out, they both married other people in the interim.

About 10 years later, by which time they were both divorced (again) and Kathleen was the mother of two children, Fate duly brought them back together and they began seeing each other again socially just before Clark left for the *Soldier of Fortune* shoot in Hong Kong in November of 1954. At this time Kathleen was only slightly older than Carole had been when she died. When Clark returned in mid–December, it was with gifts for Kathleen and the children, Joan and Bunker. From then on, they saw each other practically every day. Just as Carole had done, Kathleen made up her mind she would become part of his life and so the wealthy socialite learned how to hunt, shoot, fish, ride and play golf. She became Clark's close friend and companion; he began to rush back from the studio at nights so he would have time to read to the children before they went to bed.

In April, they faced another separation while Clark traveled south to Durango, Mexico, to work in *The Tall Men*. They were sitting by the pool at the ranch one afternoon when Clark turned to Kathleen and proposed they get married, saying he'd actually been waiting a long time to do it. Kathleen replied that she'd been waiting for him to ask so she could say yes.

Both very private people, they decided to keep their plans secret. When Clark returned from Mexico, he and Kathleen and her sister Elizabeth, along with their friends Al and Julie Menasco, drove to Minden, Nevada, where the marriage took place on July 11, 1955.

Although Clark offered to take her anywhere in the world to live, Kathleen knew how much he loved the Encino ranch. She claimed to feel no rivalry with any ghosts and so that was where they settled to live a happy, harmonious family life. It seemed to be the time for Clark's life to be this way and, when all is said and done, that is the right time.

183 The very model of a 1950s house-wife, Kathleen traveled with Clark in the early summer of 1955 to St. George, Utah, along with 80 cast and crew, for the duration of his work in *The King and Four Queens*. There the Gables rented a house where she would rise at dawn to prepare breakfast and to pack a homemade lunch for him with a flask of coffee. Then while he went off to the set, she would join a town quilting or needlepoint group, read, or go shopping. Every evening when Clark arrived back from work, she would have supper on the table after which she would return to reading or embroidering while Clark studied his lines for the next day's shooting. On days off, Clark taught her to roll her own cigarettes, or they might ride or shoot skeet together.

183 Clark and Kathleen sharing a moment while taking a meal break from *The King and Four Queens*, outside of St. George, Utah, in 1955 (courtesy the Gable Archive).

Kathleen had made few alterations in Clark's life since their marriage and that suited him just fine. He was now a man who did not like changes, especially sudden ones, and who preferred his days to roll out on schedule. Clark might not mind where he ate, but his meals came on time: lunch was at noon and supper at seven. Now that he was a family man, his work day was equally as defined; his contracts now stipulated that he finish at five. Clark was proud of the children and doted on them, spending as much time as he could with them when he wasn't working. When he did arrive home from work, Kathleen made sure her makeup was right and she had on a clean dress, that there was a drink ready and music was playing softly in the background. After all, she was both married to and custodian of a national treasure, and she took the job seriously.

184 Clark and Kathleen attending a Hollywood function (courtesy the Gable Archive).

Clark and Kathleen were both deeply in love and they had a wonderful friendship. They truly did enjoy living with each other.

184 It was Kathleen who persuaded Clark to again begin attending major social functions, something that he had basically preferred not to do since Carole died. In late October 1956, they appeared at the Hollywood premiere of *Giant* to which they drove in Clark's new 300SL Mercedes Cabriolet. The following year they began to travel together, and in March 1958 they were seen at the premiere of *Teacher's Pet* with Kathleen in a black satin Mainbocher gown and matching stole.

That year, Clark was persuaded to appear at the 30th Annual Academy Awards at the RKO Pantages Theatre as a co-presenter of the Writing Awards with Doris Day, who had co-starred with him in *Teacher's Pet*. They were introduced by Bob Hope to present the Award for Story and Screenplay Written Directly for the Screen to George Wells for *Designing Woman* and for Screenplay Based on Material from Another Medium to Pierre Boulle (Kim Novak accepted on his behalf) but not to Michael Wilson or Carl Foreman, who had been blacklisted, for their work on *The Bridge on the River Kwai*. Soon after, Clark and Kathleen left for Chicago, Cleveland and Washington, DC, on a rare promotional tour for *Teacher's Pet*. While touring the White House, they were invited by President Eisenhower to visit his office and chat.

In July of 1960, Clark and Kathleen asked Al and Julie Menasco to meet them in Minden, Nevada, on the way to Reno where they would stay while *The Misfits* was being shot, to celebrate the Gables' fifth wedding anniversary. As the Menascos waited under the same cottonwood trees where they had stood five years before, looking south down the road, they saw Clark and Kathleen chugging towards them in an old Model T Ford they had rented with Kathleen nursing the celebratory champagne. As they ground to a halt, Al looked up, shaking his head. "When does the honeymoon end?" he asked in bemusement. "Never," answered Kathleen with a laugh. "With us — never."

Four months later Clark was gone.

185　　Bunker and his stepfather Clark became close friends during the few years they knew each other. Both children adored their stepfather, and would sit out in the driveway to wait for him when he arrived home from the studio shortly after five in the evening. Never known by his given name of Adolph Spreckels III, Bunker (or "Bunks" as his mother called him) was only five when Kathleen and Clark were married.

When he was sent to St. John's Military Academy across town, Clark affectionately dubbed him "General." Clark taught him a lot about survival in the outdoors, riding, shooting, swimming, fishing, even handling a lasso. When Bunker joined the Encino Little League, Clark spent hours practicing with him. He also taught him about reading and words; Clark had his gun cases ripped out and replaced with bookcases, and he had a large Webster's unabridged dictionary mounted on a stand in which he taught Bunker to search for the meanings of words.

Bunker had an exclusive education that could have prepared him for diplomatic or financial careers, but he wanted to go into the Air Force and fly. He became sidetracked by the sixties, though, preferring in the end to become part of the surfing and drug culture in California. When he turned 18, Bunker left for Hawaii, effectively turning his back on both families. Although he could have made much of the Spreckel contacts with Hawaiian royalty, not to mention being regarded as a reincarnated Hawaiian prince, he preferred to live a monastic life there enhanced by hallucinogens that he felt aided him to be one with the ocean.

Bunker was the heir to the Spreckels sugar fortune through his grandmother because his father pre-deceased her. When he turned 21 he inherited $50,000,000 that, so the story goes, he promptly withdrew from the bank in cash and took away in an armored car to be stored in a secret cave.

During the early seventies he began to experiment with creative surfboard design, shortening and reshaping boards, along with creative methods of riding them; at one time, he estimated he owned 39 boards. However, his life began to unravel under the impact of unlimited wealth from his inheritance and a hedonistic lifestyle with few boundaries. He set up residences in various hotels around the world and became legendary for his excesses.

Still, Bunker was very artistic and by the mid-seventies was involved in a number of projects involving film and music. He felt ready to retire from surfing, and he was working on a film of his own as well as the Lucifer Rising project with director Kenneth Anger. In late 1976, he claimed that he would be ideal for the role of Lucifer because he'd once met Satan personally and they had discussed Bunker's future. Satan, he declared, didn't scare him.

It was probably just as well. Bunker died suddenly and mysteriously in Hawaii on January 7, 1977.

185　The handsome young boy on the right is Bunker Spreckels Gable, with his sister Joan, already looking as though he belongs in the water (courtesy the Gable Archive).

Epilogue

186–187　*Clark Gable in Mansfield*

186　Delma Northern (left) and future GI bride Mavis Pollard (right) photographed with Clark.

His playboy presence was a flickering flame,
dazzling with diamond-bracelet smiles.
GABLE MOBBED BY FANS WHO TRAVELLED MILES
the papers said we put New York to shame,
but Mansfield fans set up a waiting game
and got him signing photographs in piles.
Fire-lipped typists, abandoning their files
mobbed him for copies of his well-heeled name.
"Clark, over here, Clark"— Still that refrain clings,
"mi Mam thinks you're the dishiest man alive!"
Still I see him, standing hand in pocket,
as if Mansfield was glamorous Palm Springs
and not a place to make his spirits dive.

I keep him like a picture in a locket.

for Martyn

Deborah Tyler-Bennett

With permission, from her collection *Clark Gable in Mansfield:
Selected Poems* (Kings England: Rotherham, UK, 2003).

CLARK GABLE

THE KING OF HOLLYWOOD

William Clarke Gable, stage and motion picture actor, was born at Cadiz, Ohio, on February 1, 1901, in a house that once stood on this site. He was reared in nearby Hopedale. During his film career of 36 years, Gable made 67 talking pictures including **It Happened One Night** *for which he won an Oscar in 1934 as Best Actor and the classic* **Gone With The Wind** *which won the Academy Award for Best Picture of 1939. He died November 16, 1960, in Hollywood, California.*

Dedicated February 1, 1986

187   The Clark Gable memorial in Cadiz, Ohio, near his reconstructed birthplace home.

Index